Following Jesus

Also by John J. Boucher

An Introduction to the Catholic Charismatic Renewal

Bringing Christ to My Everyday World:
Adult Catholic School of Evangelism

Bringing Prayer Meetings to Life

Christian Marriage: Sacrament of Abiding Friendship

Finding God in the Workplace (Audio tapes)

Simple Ways Catholics Can Share Faith in Everyday Life

The Healing Mass Project:
A New Strategy for Catholic Evangelization

Following Jesus

A Disciple's Guide to Discerning God's Will

John J. Boucher

Dove Publications
Pecos, New Mexico

Published by Dove Publications
Pecos, NM 87552
(505) 757-6597

(Following Jesus is a revised edition of the book previously titled, *Is Talking to God a Long-Distance Call?* ISBN-0-89283-669-5.)

Cover design by John Murello
Book Layout by Document Design Computer Service

ACKNOWLEDGMENTS

Scripture text used in this work are taken from *New American Bible with Revised New Testament*, Copyright © 1986, Confraternity of Christian Doctrine, Washington, D.C., 20017 and are used with permission of copyright owner. All rights reserved.

Contents

For Therese
on our twenty-fifth wedding anniversary

Introduction

"YOU CAN HEAR FROM GOD!" Sister Mary Frances exhorted her class of sixth graders. Paul didn't believe it. God might have spoken to prophets or apostles. That was a long, long time ago. He dismissed the thought and filed it away with other unimportant information adults could be so intense about.

Then one night when Paul was twenty he found himself surrounded by thick, black air behind the mess tent. There was a lot to wonder about. He had pulled guard duty on the western perimeter of an army base near Da Nang, South Vietnam. Even though he had a relatively safe job as a cook, the hell around him and a worsening drug habit had turned life sour. He repositioned himself against a wall of burlap sacks filled with rice, as if to clear his mind.

Suddenly the night exploded around him. Incoming machine gun fire pierced his emotional funk. Paul dropped to the ground. When the shooting had stopped, he crawled back to his post to have a look around. That's when he noticed that the burlap bags had been peppered with bullet holes. His head had rested against them seconds before the firing started.

The hair on his neck stood straight up. Sweat traced icy fingers down his spine. Clear as the starting buzzer for a basketball game, he heard Sr. Mary Frances' voice, "You can hear from God!" That wasn't all he heard. Words formed in his mind, "Because I love you, none of these bullets had your name on it." Paul was converted to a living faith in Jesus Christ. Since then he has been able to live drug-free, and settle into a happy marriage. He has especially enjoyed opportunities to teach religion classes in his parish.

You can hear from God too! You don't have to go to Vietnam, nor even leave your home. Millions of Christians hear God's voice in their daily lives. Beth, for example, simply listens for one line of Scripture at Sunday Mass and writes it down on a slip of paper right there in the pew. Then she sticks it on her refrigerator with an apple magnet for a few days.

An important first step is to realize that God is always speaking to you out of immeasurable love. In Part One of *Following Jesus: A Disciple's Guide to Discerning God's Will,* we will take a look at how you can grow in awareness of God's voice. What seems like a tiny whisper in a sea of noises can be amplified. The Lord offers you a hearing aid, even ear surgery, whatever you need to hear and understand. Let the Spirit within you highlight the meaning of words that you read in Scripture, of the events going on around you, or even of a friend's kindness.

My wife Therese once spent three hundred dollars on an overseas phone call to Thailand in order to straighten out a relationship with her former fiancé. Jesus has paid much more than three hundred dollars to talk to you. God will bridge any distance, healing any deafness you experience. Jesus, the Word of God, spent every ounce of his strength to call out to you in love.

Part Two will explore channels for hearing God that Christians have relied on throughout history. God speaks through human wisdom and a sense of your personal spiritual identity, through prophetic messages, the lives of saints and others, the Scriptures, and through the church. Paul's experience in Vietnam with a prophetic message may seem unusual, but God's voice rings clear with many small yet unmistakable syllables. Do you choose as many of these channels for hearing God's voice as your daily life allows? The Lord's word is meant to sustain you like a mighty stream of fresh, cool water.

Part Three outlines attitudes like faithfulness, teachableness, and detachment that you can cultivate in order to live a life open to God's voice. Without them your heart and mind may remain behind closed doors, inaccessible to the Lord who is always knocking. Without them you could read Scripture for six hours a day and walk away without experiencing the peace, joy, and consolation that leap out at you from God's word. Fostering these attitudes will bear fruit in your relationship with Jesus and will overflow into family life and friendships as well.

Part Four will offer guidelines for testing specific inspirations and promptings from God. It will focus on the criteria for discerning the spiritual source of a message: common sense, God-directedness, a deeper love for others, living the cross, poverty, detachment, unity with the church, obedience, sound doctrine, and opposition to the world. You will learn concrete ways to respond to authentic inspirations and promptings. Finally, you will be shown a simple four-step process for making a decision based on God's messages to you: daily relationship, deliberation, decision, and doing.

Following Jesus will offer many helpful insights for everyday people. To gain the most from what is offered, you may want to underline key words and read it slowly as a workbook, answering the questions under **Personal Reflection** in the space indicated at the end of each chapter. A further challenge to growth is offered for those who choose to do the optional activities under **Practical Application**.

Small groups can use the book together and consider the questions For **Small Group Sharing** or **Further Reflection** that end each chapter. Space has been provided for your answers. You will find it a useful tool for your small group, whether it be a gathering for study, prayer, Bible sharing, RENEW, faith sharing, or the Catechumenate/RCIA (Rite of Christian Initiation of Adults). You may use the following simple approach or adapt it as needed:

1. Gather a group of eight to fifteen people in a home or at church. Discuss using this book as a group for thirteen or fourteen meetings.

2. Decide to meet weekly, biweekly, or monthly for one-and-a-half hours.

3. Agree on what chapter you will read at home before the next meeting. Encourage one another to consider the personal reflection questions and even to try the practical application in your daily life. Encourage each other to come to meetings,

whether or not you always get a chance to read the assigned chapter or go over reflection questions.

4. Before you gather, your leader should choose two or three of the small group sharing questions from the chapter to focus the group discussion. Quite often, however, just asking people what struck them from the chapter will be all you need to get started.

5. Try the following schedule for your meetings, or adapt it as needed:

  ● Five minutes—Opening prayer and brief Scripture reading (choose a reading quoted in the chapter);

  ● Thirty minutes—Discussion, using **For Small Group Sharing** or **Further Reflection**;

  ● Fifteen to thirty minutes—Sharing, based on **Personal Reflection** and/or **Practical Application**;

  ● Five to ten minutes—Prayer aloud together for personal needs, perhaps followed by a closing song;

  ● Twenty minutes—Informal time, including refreshments if desired.

6. Remember that everything discussed should be held in confidence, so that real openness and accountability are possible.

A depressed young man once lay in the hospital, dying from leukemia. A friend encouraged him to imagine Jesus sitting on the chair beside his bed. The friend encouraged him to talk to the Lord as well. As the dying man spoke with Jesus this way each day, he experienced great hope. The nurse who found him dead one morning was deeply moved by the joyous peace on his face. His head rested on the chair next to his hospital bed. That's the kind of openness God wants us to have with him and each other, as brothers and sisters.

You can talk to God, you can hear from God today! The Lord yearns to speak to you, to lean closer and fill your heart. Jesus is waiting, and he is more than equal to the task.

Part One

God Is
Always Speaking

ONE

You Can Hear from God Today!

I WAS STUNNED. After five weeks of taking accordion lessons, I couldn't play as well as my teacher, Mr. Proia. My ten-year-old mind could not fathom the possibility that some things take time. Mr. Proia encouraged me to keep going. He whispered, "Surrender to the process. Let the instrument become part of your everyday life. It will grow on you, like another hand or foot." After a year of struggling, I quit.

Years later it happened again. I was stunned. After five months of trying to live an intense Christian life, I couldn't figure out what God's will was for me. My twenty-two-year-old mind could not fathom the possibility that some things take time. A few directions from a retreat talk kept me from quitting. Fr. Bill encouraged me: "1) Surrender to God; 2) Study how to know the Lord's will; 3) Get support for your spiritual life; 4) Be very patient." I needed to open avenues that would let me hear from God. "The first word God says to you is 'HEAR'" (St. Ambrose, Italy, 340-397).[1]

SURRENDER TO GOD

First, God calls you to make a complete gift of self to Jesus, to surrender in trust. If you have not asked Jesus Christ to be the Lord and center of your life, now is the time to do so. Then you need to ask God for a full release of the Holy Spirit through the graces of your baptism and confirmation, so that you may be empowered to follow him more closely.

For some this complete gift of self is made with certainty like the crack of a whip at a particular moment in their lives. Noel Paul

Stookey, of the folksingers "Peter, Paul, and Mary," heard God's call in 1968 through a young stranger:

> When I saw him after the show, I said, "What is it you'd like to talk to me about?" He looked me right in the eyes. He said, "I want to talk to you about God."... I'm fascinated. He talked about how, through the dramatic intervention of the Holy Spirit, he now had a personal relationship with Jesus Christ and what that meant. I kept drawing connections between what I was looking for in my life and what had happened in his life.... When the opportunity came to talk to God in a prayerful position, I just started to cry. I realized at that moment, as I said I was sorry, that I was confessing not only a distance from God, but confessing all the excesses of my life as well. The following morning, I was a new person.[2]

For others, like my wife Therese, this call from God has grown slowly like a beautiful flower in a well-kept garden. Her parents prayed for several years to have a child, and rejoiced at her birth. But their faith was tested when the obstetrician discovered her clubbed foot. A temporary cast was put on her leg, and surgery was scheduled. Meanwhile her parents brought her to the shrine of St. Frances Xavier Cabrini in New York City to pray for healing. When the doctor removed the cast from her foot several months later, her condition had been healed.

She recalls many times while growing up when she offered herself to God: First Communion, at daily Mass with her mother, during a particular song by the church choir, and on retreats. Each experience has been a further unfolding of the petals of God's life in her. Her adult journey in the power of the Holy Spirit has led her to be a devoted wife and mother, a published author, and a skilled religious educator.

Prayer: Daily Gift of Self to God. Jesus calls you to offer your life as a daily gift to him. The normal way to accomplish this is through regular daily personal prayer and meditation. Why not start with fifteen to thirty minutes? Make an effort to come before the Lord. In God's presence you become available to him, ready to obey his Word.

This is what St. Peter was doing when God showed him in a

vision that Gentiles, as well as Jews, were meant to enter the kingdom of God. He saw a vision of a sheet filled with all sorts of animals:

> A voice said to him, "Get up, Peter. Slaughter and eat." But Peter said, "Certainly not, sir. For never have I eaten anything profane and unclean." The voice spoke to him again, a second time, "What God has made clean, you are not to call profane." (Acts 10:13-15)

It was from this prayer experience that Peter had the assurance to preach the gospel to Cornelius and his household. Cornelius himself had sent for Peter after receiving a vision while praying (Acts 10:1-8).

Of course God probably will not speak through visions and voices in your daily prayer. Still, the Holy One is speaking. Today the Lord is already speaking to you by your choosing to read *Following Jesus*. You want to hear from the Lord. God readily responds to such an opening.

Alice shares that desire with you. She has noticed that after she spends time in prayer focusing on God, for his own sake, her concern shifts to particular family members, friends, or neighbors. When she has visited or called them later in the day she has often discovered that they had some illness, or important personal need. Alice has learned to pay attention to the people brought to mind during prayer. God is speaking to her that way. She spends part of her time interceding for God to help them in whatever they are facing at that time.

Michelle works in sales for a manufacturer. Each morning before work she spends half an hour praying with the Scripture readings for daily Mass. Any words, thoughts, phrases, or images that strike her or puzzle her she jots down in her spiritual journal. When she later reviews these notes she finds that patterns develop. Certain themes recur over a period of months which speak clearly to her about important events in her life.

With the help of her spiritual director, she has come to pay attention to these recurring thoughts and to ask God's help clarifying what this means for her life. For three months whenever the word "serve" appeared, she felt drawn to offer herself in a new way to serve in the church. When her parish's director of religious education described the urgent need for teachers in the confirmation program, Michelle was ready to volunteer. The philosopher Soren Kierkegaard once wrote, "When you read God's Word, you must constantly be saying to yourself, 'It is talking to me and about me.'"

Taking Time to Listen. The chief element of surrender to God in prayer is listening for God's voice. You must make your inner ear attentive to whatever ways the Lord may wish to speak. Humbly welcome the people, events, thoughts, images, and words that God brings to your attention. At the same time, beware of distractions. Ask yourself if the thoughts and images that come to mind lead you into prayer or take your focus off the Lord.

You are invited to wait in silence, discovering in the ordinary stuff of life the invitation of the eternal.

As much as half of your daily personal prayer could be spent listening. You might start with trying to listen for only five minutes a day. Slowly increase the time over the months and years as the Lord leads you. Through listening prayer you can discover that God wants your happiness and wholeness. You will be able to let go of self-imposed burdens:

> The more we wait upon his word, the more we experience its power to rid us of false expectations of what we think will fulfill us so that we may come to rejoice in what God is offering: the gift of himself.[3]

STUDY HOW TO KNOW GOD'S WILL

Catholics can be tempted to seek God's will through occult practices, horoscopes, New Age, and Eastern religions. Therein lie seductive temptations to get quick spiritual fixes or black-and-white immediate answers to your every question. Avoid these false ways of seeking the divine will. The search for fast, easy spiritual answers can leave you wide open to selfish desires and the wiles of the devil.

You have already inherited a great treasure. You can know Jesus and his will in the Scriptures, tradition, and teaching of the church. To receive this treasure, all you have to do is open your mind and heart through the gift of sacred study. You can find God's will right at your fingertips, at home within the body of Christ.

Study of Scripture. Sacred study includes but goes beyond the academic nature of secular study. Suppose you wanted to study a particular Scripture passage in depth. Academic study would help you to understand the sources and original meaning of the passage. This is essential. Sacred study continues by taking the academic findings and probing to interpret the meaning of the passage for today's world. More specifically, how can you apply the meaning of the passage in your everyday life? Sacred study demands that you take time to reflect on the meaning of the passage.

In ancient times such study was recognized as an important part of the life of God's people. Jews who wished to study God's law (the Torah) would attach themselves to a great and wise rabbi. They would learn of God's will from him. They would let the Torah mold their lives:

> Make me understand the way of your precepts,
>   and I will meditate on your wondrous deeds....
> I will run the way of your commands
>   when you give me a docile heart.   (Ps 119:27, 32)

Study helps you follow the way of the Lord instead of the way of falsehood. It is itself a gift from God. As you study, God grants "a docile heart," the gift of being teachable.

When you study believers portrayed in the Hebrew Scriptures, they help shape you as a follower of Yahweh. From Abraham, for instance, you learn total trust in the promises of God. He began to doubt God's promise of an heir and wondered if the child of a concubine would be good enough:

> "No, that one shall not be your heir...." [God] took him outside and said, "Look up at the sky and count the stars, if you can. Just so... shall your descendants be." Abraham put his faith in the LORD....   (Gn 15:4-6)

From others, like Ruth, you can learn the depths of covenant love. She was a Gentile. She married into the people of Israel. Naomi, Ruth's mother-in-law, told her to go back to her own people after her husband's death:

> But Ruth said, "Do not ask me to abandon or forsake you! for wherever you go I will go, wherever you lodge I will lodge, your people shall be my people, and your God my God." (Ruth 1:16)

Jesus Christ comes as the walking will of God, the fulfillment of God's covenant in the New Testament. His teaching, preaching, and miracles speak. By coming into deeper relationship with the Son, you come to know the Father. For whoever has seen Jesus has seen the Father (Jn 14:7-9). John the Evangelist tells us: "For the Father loves his Son and shows him everything that he himself does, and he will show him greater works than these, so that you may be amazed" (Jn 5:20).

This sacred study is not mere intellectual speculation about Christ and his teachings or about the Israelites who came before him. You are an apprentice learning God's ways from Jesus, master apprentice of the Father. By striving to follow Christ's teachings you can enter into a whole new life in the power of the Holy Spirit.

Drawing Upon the Treasury of the Church in Study. Along with the Scriptures, you can also draw from the treasury of the living tradition of your church about knowing and doing God's will. Tradition consists of the creeds, councils, lives of the saints, preaching, and teaching, the fruit of two thousand years of following Christ. Tradition is something like a best friend's spiritual journal. Creeds form the superstructure of faith and practice. The Apostles' Creed, for example, is not just a dusty statement from the past, but a living foundation for knowing God's will. "I believe in God, the Father Almighty, Creator of heaven and earth," sets a framework meant to guide your actions today. If God is Creator of all, then you belong to him, along with all the earth. You are called to manage his gifts to you.

Actions like polluting the environment, abortion, sexual exploitation, racism, crime, and the nuclear arms race are to be examined in the light of the Father's original plan. Whatever lessens or destroys what the Creator has given is forbidden.

Councils, such as Vatican II in the 1960s, also help you to

know God's will today. Like the firing of thrusters on a space shuttle launch, councils serve to give course corrections and new direction to the church of the present age. Vatican Council II was not called primarily to renew the religious life, to put Mass in the vernacular, or to do away with Friday fasting. It was called to prepare the church to evangelize the modern world of the twentieth and twenty-first centuries.

Church teaching, especially through the bishops and pope, offers further understanding and application of the messages of Scripture and tradition with regard to God's will. For example, Vatican Council II reminds you that all are the church together with the hierarchy. Popes Paul VI and John Paul II draw the conclusion that lay people, religious, and clergy are therefore all called to the church's mission to evangelize:

> The entire mission of the church, then, is concentrated and manifested in evangelization. Through the winding passages of history the church has made her way under the grace and the command of Jesus Christ: "Go into all the world and preach the Gospel to the whole creation" (Mk. 16:15).... "To evangelize," writes Paul VI, "is the grace and vocation proper to the church, her most profound identity."[4]

For the Catholic who seeks to know God's will, the question is never, "Should I evangelize or not?" but rather "Lord, can you show me how to evangelize? Show me where to start."

The Saints. Lives of the saints are another major resource for Christian study. Canonization is official recognition of heroic knowing and doing of God's will. Not to read and study saints' lives today is to miss the treasure in your own spiritual home, the body of Christ. There are gleaming golden coins of spiritual wisdom in overwhelming abundance:

> Cast yourself into the arms of God and be very sure that if He wants anything of you, He will fit you for the work and give you strength. (St. Philip Neri, Italy, 1515-1595)[5]

> Our body is not made of iron. Our strength is not that of stone. Live and hope in the Lord, and let your service be according to

reason. Modify your holocaust with the salt of prudence. (St. Clare of Assisi, Italy, 1194-1253)[6]

I pray God may open your eyes and let you see what hidden treasures he bestows on us in the trials from which the world only thinks to flee. (St. John of Avila, Spain, 1499-1569)[7]

Mature Christians know that faithfulness to the study of Scripture, tradition, and church teaching counts more than the amount of time spent each day. More than twenty years ago I decided to spend twenty minutes a day in study. I split my time into three sections in order to read two pages of a Catholic magazine, two pages of a serious spiritual growth book, and finally a chapter of Scripture each day. By God's grace I have remained faithful to this little study plan. Such study has become an empowering habit in the Holy Spirit.[8]

Finally, it is important to learn from your own experience. God can give you a kind of "sanctified common sense." You need to take time to reflect on nature, on God's creation, and on your daily Christian life. God can teach you how to know and do his will through successes and failures, through your relationships with others, and even through the experiences of society and culture:

All the things in this world are gifts of God, created for us, to be the means by which we can come to know him better, [and] love him more surely.... As a result, we ought to appreciate and use these gifts as they help us toward our goal of loving service.... Our only desire and our only choice should be that option which better leads us to the goal for which God has created us. (St. Ignatius Loyola, Spain, 1491-1556)[9]

SUPPORT FOR YOUR SPIRITUAL LIFE

Share with Spiritual Friends. Among the many gifts of God are other Christians. In order to know God's will you are called to enter into a supportive network of relationships. During one of the most difficult periods of my life, I attempted to teach religion in a Catholic high school. I was not prepared for the intense resistance to faith and gospel that many of my three hundred students expressed. Four sets of Christian relationships bore me up through the daily fears and anxieties which I experienced: the spiritual friendship of my wife, the wise guidance of my spiritual director, the patience and love of our small prayer and Bible sharing group, and the encouragement of fellow parishioners at our Sunday morning liturgies. Each of these Christian relationships helped me to know God's will and to live it during that time and afterward.

Anyone seeking God's will would want to develop as many of these sets of Christian support relationships in his or her life as possible. The first relationship is that of spiritual friend. Human beings have an authentic need for friendship and intimacy. However, it isn't possible to have more than a few intimate friends.

Jesus' closest spiritual friends seem to have been Peter, James, and John. He took them up the mountain for the transfiguration, and also to Gethsemane for prayer before his death. John is presented as the "beloved disciple" with whom Jesus would share everything. We find him eating at Jesus' right side during the Last Supper. The Lord even left his mother in John's care as he hung upon the cross. Spiritual friendship involves sharing, witnessing, challenging, and praying. You need someone with whom you can share "gut" feelings, not just beliefs or information. It means becoming truly vulnerable to another. "Friend: Someone who knows all about you, and loves you just the same" (St. Augustine, N. Africa, 354-430).[10]

Such a relationship provides a sounding board for what God is doing in your life, and especially what's happening in your prayer life. Whenever I have needed to talk, my friend Dick has been available. I recall many times when we have gone fishing in his canoe just to be alone and share about the Lord. He has taught me how to relax and play together as Christians. Recreation with such a brother or sister in Jesus has become a true "re-creation" of my inner being.

You need someone to share prayer with in an intimate way. Long before I fell in love with my wife Therese, I used to drive her and other women home from a weekly college faith-sharing group. The very first thing that attracted me to her was that she was willing to pray with me before I dropped her off. She was willing to spend time praying about our individual and families' needs. Such prayer has continued to cement the spiritual friendship at the heart of our marriage over the past twenty-five years.

Spiritual Direction. Another important Christian relationship that may guide you in the direction of God's will is one formed with a spiritual director. A spiritual director is someone more advanced in the Christian life, with whom you can discuss your spiritual growth on a regular basis. The aim is not counseling for emotional problems or reception of the sacrament of penance. If a good director realizes you need professional counseling, he or she will recommend someone. Since confession is not the goal of spiritual direction, your spiritual director need not be a priest. Many priests today are not trained, nor do they feel able to give spiritual direction. On the other hand, many religious and lay people are gifted and trained to give spiritual direction. It is suggested that you meet with a spiritual director on a monthly or bimonthly basis for about an hour. Since the person you meet with may be doing spiritual direction as part of their livelihood, it is just to offer a donation equivalent to an hour's wage each time you meet.

Spiritual direction has the following purposes: 1) to teach you how to receive direction from Jesus and the Holy Spirit; 2) to mirror or reflect back to you what God seems to be doing in your life; 3) to offer checks and balances on the spiritual leadings and promptings you receive (i.e., are these from God, yourself, or the evil one?); 4) to hold you accountable for decisions you make in order to follow Christ.

Three problems often keep people from forming a successful relationship with a spiritual director. First, you may want to find the "perfect spiritual director." You will not settle into such a relationship until you have searched the highways and byways for the most holy, wise, and spiritual person who exists on the face of the earth. The result is that you never get spiritual direction. St. Therese of Lisieux (France, 1873-1897) suggests that it is better to take the spiritual director who is available to you over not having a spiritual director at all.

The second temptation is "shopping around" for a person who always agrees with you. Quite frankly, if your spiritual director cannot disagree with you, you probably have the wrong spiritual director. You cannot grow in the spiritual life if you cannot be contradicted and corrected. You end up giving spiritual direction to yourself. Surely, you do not believe your will is already in perfect conformity with God's will?

Humility is the foundation of all the other virtues. It is so necessary for perfection that, among all the ways to reach it, the first is humility, the second is humility, and the third is still humility. And if I were asked about it one hundred times, I would still give the same answer. (St. Augustine, N. Africa, 354-430)[11]

Third, you will be tempted to "intimidate" your spiritual director at times. Rigid statements like "God told me to do this" or "The Blessed Virgin wants this" are intimidation. A much more submissive and Christian approach is to say, "Well, this is what I think God may be saying, but what do you think?" Then you are not trying to put a spiritual director in the untenable position of: 1) disagreeing with God or 2) feeling obliged to tell you just how prideful you sound. St. Teresa of Avila (Spain, 1515-1582) made it a practice not to speak of leadings and promptings she received as coming directly from God at all. She would rephrase even direct commands from God as, "Well, I've been wondering if I should do this or respond in that way." She would give the spiritual director freedom to correct her.

Where can you find a spiritual director? Go to a local parish, convent, or retreat house and ask if anyone there gives spiritual direction. If not, then ask staff members or mature Catholics around you where they go to get spiritual direction. When you have found someone, stay with that person at least four to six months before deciding to make it a more permanent relationship. Some people find it helpful to have a spiritual director from outside of their parish or community setting, for the sake of objective input about important decisions or ministry. In this case, there is also a disadvantage. The spiritual director does not see you functioning in a community setting, making it more difficult to compare your perceptions of yourself with what is really happening.

Spiritual Support Groups. Small groups of believing Catholics (eight to twenty people) are an important avenue for discovering God's will. There are many small weekly or biweekly faith-sharing groups, where you can experience community and mutual support. Many spiritual renewal movements foster such sharing: Marriage Encounter image groups, RENEW Bible-sharing groups, Little Rock

Scripture Study groups, and charismatic prayer groups are just a few. Become part of such a community and be faithful. You will grow in hearing God speak.

The Liturgical Assembly. A second kind of sharing happens when people gather with other Catholics at Sunday liturgy, the sacrament of reconciliation, and other sacramental and liturgical celebrations. Through the preaching, the proclamation of God's Word, and the physical symbols and actions of worship, you are formed as part of the people of God. You learn how to "think with the Church" (St. Ignatius Loyola, Spain, 1491-1556).

BE VERY PATIENT

Hearing and doing God's will are part of a lifelong process of surrender, study, and sharing. This process requires patience with yourself and with God. The modern "instant gratification" or "vending machine" mentality is terribly offended by the slow pace at which you grow in the Lord. You will make mistakes. Do not fear. Boldly repent and go on, knowing that Jesus is more interested in leading you than you are in seeking his leadings:

> God has created me
> to do Him some definite service.
> He has committed some work to me
> which He has not committed to another.
> I have my mission.
> I may not know what it is in this life.
> But I shall be told in the next.
> I am a link in a chain,
> a bond of connection between persons.
> He has not created me for nothing.
> I shall do good. I shall do His work.
> Therefore I will trust Him.
> Whatever I do, wherever I am, I cannot be thrown away.
> If I am in sickness, my sickness may serve Him.
> If I am in sorrow, my sorrow may serve Him.
> He does nothing in vain. He knows what He is about.
> (Cardinal John Henry Newman, England, 1801-1890)[12]

FOR REFLECTION, APPLICATION, AND DISCUSSION

Personal Reflection:

1. In your life, has the call to a complete gift of self to God been more like a clap of thunder or the gradual unfolding of flower petals? Why?

2. Chart and describe your present efforts to grow in surrender, study, and sharing as avenues for knowing God's will. How do your present efforts and future plans compare to one another? Which plans do you consider most important right now?

Category	Present Efforts	Feelings	Future Plans
Surrender			
Study			
Sharing			

3. What is it that keeps you from quitting in your growth as a Christian? Use this as a survey question to ask a half-dozen of your Catholic friends. List their responses below:

Name: Response to the survey question:

a. _____

b. _____

c. _____

d. _____

e. _____

f. _____

Practical Application:

Selecting and maintaining a relationship with a spiritual director can prove to be one of the most difficult efforts in your Christian life. Look for the seeds of the following in someone you are considering to be your spiritual director:

1. Charism or gift of spiritual direction recognized by the church and other mature Christians.

2. Can teach others how to let the Holy Spirit lead.

3. Openness to others; unconditional love and wisdom.

4. Knowledge of the spiritual life.

 a. head knowledge—
  well-rounded intellectual grasp

 b. heart knowledge—
  spiritually experienced and maturing.

Make an appointment this week to see a spiritual director.

For Small Group Sharing or Further Reflection:

1. Describe a time when you made a complete gift of yourself to God. How has this affected your relationships with family, friends, and fellow workers?

2. "We are apprentices learning God's ways from Jesus, master apprentice of the Father." Do you agree or disagree with this statement? Why?

3. Sharing with others is an important part of the process of knowing God's will. Which of the support relationships described in this chapter (spiritual friendship, spiritual director, small faith sharing groups, or sacramental celebration) have offered you the most help? What is it about this kind of support that you appreciate the most?

4. "To be a saint, one must be beside oneself. One must lose one's head" (St. John Vianney, France, 1786-1859).[13] What is your reaction to this statement? Is it true for you or for other Christians you know?

5. Patience is a key to experiencing God's ongoing word to you. Who is the most patient person you know? What do you think is the key to his or her patience? How could you grow in this area?

TWO

Why God Wants to Speak to You

GOD CHOOSES TO CALL YOU FIRST. You can answer or you can put him on hold. You can doubt that God wants to speak to you. You can even forget or reject what the Lord says to you. No matter. The Lord of the universe is not diminished by your response and continues to call out to you in love.

A tale from the desert fathers of Egypt illustrates the availability of God's voice to you. The story is one of many from the fourth and fifth centuries about Abba John, a Christian hermit who fled to the solitude of the desert after Christianity became the official religion of the Roman Empire. Eventually, multitudes flocked to this holy monk, each seeking to receive a word from the Lord through him.

There was an old hermit, very ascetical in body and holy in spirit, but somewhat unclear in his thoughts. This man went to see Abba John to ask him about forgetfulness. Having received a word of wisdom, he returned to his cell. But on the way back he forgot what Abba John had told him.

So he went back and got the same word. But once again, on the way back to his cell, he forgot it. This happened several times. He would listen to Abba John and, on his way back to the cell, would be overcome by forgetfulness.

Many days later he happened to meet Abba John and he said, "Do you know, Father, that I have once again forgotten what you told me? I would have come back again but I have been enough of a bother to you already and do not want to overburden you."

Abba John said to him, "Go and light a lamp." The old man

lit the lamp. Then John said, "Bring in some more lamps and light them from the first one." This, too, the man did.

Then Abba John said to the old man, "Did the first lamp suffer any loss from the fact that the other lamps were lit from it?"

"No," said the old man.

"Well, then, so it is with me. If not only you but the whole town of Scetis were to come to me to seek help or advice, I would not suffer the slightest loss. So come to me whenever you wish, without hesitation".[1]

Abba John's image of the lamp from which other lamps are lit offers a picture of the compassion and love God has for those who strain their inner ears to hear the divine voice. What picture do you have of God? Do you believe the Lord speaks to you? If you do, are you moved with gratitude and a desire to please God? Whenever you are ready to listen, God is ready to speak.

The Father speaks with a five-fold purpose: 1) to deepen your sense of his presence—assuring you of his love and forgiveness near at hand in all circumstances; 2) to encourage and console you—helping you to see life's joys and sorrows through his eyes; 3) to guide you—showing you his will in everyday life; 4) to build up the church—revealing to you all your spiritual gifts so that you may serve the church and the world; 5) to predict the future—preparing you to respond to the Lord's call or turning you back toward him and away from sin.

TO DEEPEN YOUR SENSE OF THE LORD'S PRESENCE

A young mother sent her preschool daughter out in the back yard to play. The child was fine in the yard alone as long as she could be assured her mother was within hearing range. As the busy woman hustled about her daily tasks, her daughter would call out every fifteen minutes, "Mom, are you there?" The mother replied, "Yes dear! I'm right here!" The child was at peace.

You are like the preschool child. In your everyday life you need the assurance that God the Father is still present. God met that need by sending his Son Jesus in human flesh. Today he speaks to you through Scripture and prayer and touches you through the sacraments and other people. Thus, Christ is incarnate in our midst in Word and sacrament:

> "Behold, the virgin shall be with child and bear a son, and they shall name him Emmanuel," which means "God is with us" (Mt 1:23).

Through his death and resurrection Christ assures you that his love is too strong to leave you orphaned. He is risen. As if this weren't enough, you are also given his Spirit in the very fiber of your deepest inner self:

> For if I do not go, the Advocate will not come to you. But if I go, I will send him to you. (Jn 16:7)

> And behold, I am with you always, until the end of the age. (Mt 28:20)

God can deepen your sense of his presence in the ordinary routine of everyday life. My last two days have been clouded with discouragement. For a week I have been confined to the house on crutches following knee surgery. I feel so helpless, dependent, and useless. The smallest tasks are beyond me. This morning my wife urged me to go with her and the children to a cookout at a friend's house.

To lighten my mood, God is calling me through her to go outside myself and visit others. God knows what I need more than I do. By listening and obeying now, I will later recognize the Lord's voice as familiar.

Since you are human, you have the freedom to turn away from God's presence partially or entirely. Often, even daily, God calls you to return to him, to repent of sin and selfishness separating you from him and from others. King David ordered Uriah (husband of Bathsheba) to battle where he would be killed. God called David back to his senses through the prophet Nathan, who likened David to a man who slaughtered the single lamb of a poor neighbor. David recognized his serious predicament and his sin, repented from the heart, and accepted Yahweh's forgiveness (2 Sam 11-12).

God offers mercy and grace to deepen or restore your relationship with him. All you need to do is turn around and be present to receive the Lord's love once again. Barbara, an intensive care nurse, describes her sense of God's presence as much like dancing. At times you turn away from your partner, but when you turn around, the dance continues.

Barbara grew up in a Catholic home and attended Catholic schools. As a teenager she rebelled against her strict upbringing. After graduation she stopped going to church and decided to "just love people." By twenty-five she had been in several sexual relationships and was living with one of her lovers.

She explains her experience, "Each time I broke off with a guy, I would go back to church and start to pick up my life with God. Then I'd feel lonely and plunge back into the singles bar crowd and end up sleeping with another guy." Then Barbara was invited on a Marian Pilgrimage to Europe by a member of her family. At one of the shrines she felt she came to a personal relationship with Jesus Christ, and went to confession "for real," as she relates it.

Since then Barbara has steadily grown in her love of God and the church. After ten years of spiritual growth she wrote, "I've just about surrendered all ideas of getting married. I feel that God may be inviting me to live the single life for him. Last spring, I helped lead a Catholic Bible study in my parish. You know, I am really free now. Thank God!"

TO ENCOURAGE AND CONSOLE YOU

God also speaks in order to encourage and console you. After a frustrating attempt to preach the gospel in Athens, St. Paul moved on to Corinth. Soon resistance to his message arose there also. He must have been tempted to move on again. Instead the Lord appeared to him and encouraged him to preach:

> "No one will attack and harm you, for I have many people in this city." He settled there for a year and a half and taught the word of God among them. (Acts 18:10-11)

Though I haven't been encouraged by divine visions, often other people have given me strength to continue. One time, after five or six years of full-time lay ministry in the church, I was ready to quit. I brought my misgivings to my pastor for discernment. Fr.

Cyril heard me out, smiled, chuckled, and then looked me straight in the eyes.

"John," he said, "You don't see any results from your work."

I nodded.

"You can't see why you and your family should have to put up with the sacrifices of full-time ministry if this is true."

I nodded again.

"But John, that is not my experience of your ministry. It seems to me, wherever you are, something is always happening!"

His words have been an encouragement to me ever since that moment. When I'm feeling low and useless in ministry and service to others, I need to change my glasses. I need to see things not from my own perspective, asking, "Why aren't the things I want and expect to happen happening?" I need to see with God's eyes what is really happening around me.

God also wants to console you in everyday life. When my father died, I fell to pieces emotionally. Watching a vigorous man deteriorate from one hundred eighty to only ninety pounds with bone cancer gave me nightmares for months. Although I knew a great deal about helping others to grieve over a loved one's death, I could not give myself permission to cry. A few months afterward, our family participated in a religious education session about prayer in our parish. During the adult class, the leaders showed a filmstrip set to the song, "You Are Near" by Daniel L. Schutte of the St. Louis Jesuits. The words touched my troubled heart:

> Yahweh, I know you are near,
> Standing always at my side.
> You guard me from the foe,
> And you lead me in ways everlasting.[2]

As the strains of the music embraced me, I sensed God the Father and my own father embracing me, comforting me in my grief. I cried and cried, experiencing deep personal, emotional, and spiritual consolation.

TO GUIDE YOU

God speaks to guide you in your everyday life. St. Therese of Lisieux (France, 1873-1897) was extremely bothered by the bad habit of one of the other sisters. Whenever they gathered to pray, this sister started picking her nose. This distracted Therese, and eventually she brought her irritation to the Lord in prayer. God's suggestion to Therese was that she make this poor woman one of her best friends. So she did, confirming the old saying, "A saint is someone who lives out an ordinary life in an extraordinary way."

A candidate for sainthood, Fr. Solanus Casey, O.F.M., Cap. (USA, 1870-1957), lived and ministered in the Midwest and in the New York City area. Fr. Casey was a model of responding to God's guidance in daily life. After moving from one occupation to another, young Solanus Casey found his niche in life as one of the country's early electric trolley drivers. Then he witnessed a brutal stabbing in the roughest section of Superior, Wisconsin. The incident triggered a conversion in Casey. He responded by entering St. Francis Seminary in Milwaukee, Wisconsin at age twenty-two. But because of low grades, he was dismissed from the seminary in 1896.

On another inspiration from God, he applied to enter the Capuchin Order in Detroit, Michigan. He was accepted and finally ordained a priest in 1904. Fr. Casey went on to lead a life of selfless service. He brought hope and healing to the poor, sick, and suffering of Detroit and New York City during the Great Depression in the 1920s, '30s, and '40s. Thousands came to his doorway seeking counseling and prayers for spiritual, emotional, and physical illness. A blind woman named Eva, and Bertha Smith, who was dying of stomach cancer, were both healed, as well as many others.

On one occasion the brothers interrupted Fr. Casey in his ministry to ask for help. It was during the height of the Depression, and the soup kitchen that fed hundreds each day ran out of food. Fr. Casey rose and gave a simple blessing in the direction of the kitchen, then returned to the visitors surrounding his desk. Within moments a truck loaded with food appeared at the door of the kitchen. Fr. Casey's humble attitude toward God's guiding grace was challenging to all:

> Were we only to correspond to God's graces, continually being showered down on every one of us, we would be able to pass from being great sinners one day to be great saints the next.[3]

TO BUILD UP THE CHURCH

God speaks in order to build up the church. Just because you receive spiritual messages, it does not mean they are from God. Sheila grew up a Catholic, but always felt dissatisfied with her prayer experiences. At one point she read some books about New Age religion and began to incorporate elements of "spiritism" into her faith. Soon she was conducting seances to contact dead loved ones for grieving neighbors and friends.

Today Sheila is a spiritual medium and defines herself as "a satellite dish for the other world." She refuses to hear the church's or Scripture's teaching that condemns involvement in such practices. She deludes herself into thinking that she is helping people. She even leads grief-stricken priests and sisters in search of a false peace with their lost relatives. She has a two-year waiting list for her Thursday night seance. An evening with Sheila has a price tag of a thousand dollars or more.

God speaks so that you may become a servant. You do not own the Lord's messages like something bought at a store. Jesus gave you an example when he washed the apostles' feet, and he challenges you now to do the same for others:

> If I, therefore, the master and teacher, have washed your feet, you ought to wash one another's feet. I have given you a model to follow, so that as I have done for you, you should also do.
> (Jn 13:14-15)

God does not want you to settle for anything less than the Holy Spirit's voice. Don't seek the power of God, but the God of power. Don't seek voices from beyond the grave but Jesus Christ who has overcome death! Don't seek feelings of peace, but he who is Peace! Don't seek the wealth of the world, but the Lord who is your greatest treasure!

God's messages to you are distinct gifts of grace, manifestations of the love of the Holy Spirit. Such spiritual gifts are referred to in Scripture as charisms (Greek meaning free gifts of grace for service). God manifests these gifts in your life for the common good (1 Cor 12:7; 14:12), to build up Christ's body (the church on earth).

This vision of the purpose behind God's voice has been a guiding force in the life of the church throughout history. The documents of Vatican Council II reclaim this outlook for Christians:

> For the exercise of the apostolate the Holy Spirit, who sanctifies the people of God through the ministry and the sacraments, gives the faithful special gifts as well (cf. 1 Cor 12:7), "allotting them to each one as he wills" (cf. 1 Cor 12:11), so that each might place at the service of others the grace received, and become "good stewards of God's varied grace" (1 Pt 4:10), and build up thereby the whole body in charity (cf. Eph 4:16).[4]

Pope John Paul II reiterates this exhortation but cautions us as well. God's voice is not whispered in one person's ear, as if he or she lived on a desert island:

> The charisms are received in gratitude both on the part of the one who receives them and also on the part of the entire church. They are in fact a singularly rich source of grace for the vitality of the apostolate and for the holiness of the whole body of Christ, provided that they be gifts that come truly from the Spirit and are exercised in full conformity with the authentic promptings of the Spirit. In this sense the discernment of charisms is always necessary.... For this reason no charism dispenses a person from reference and submission to the pastors of the Church.[5]

Sheila's example falls clearly outside of acceptable norms. Her voices are the spirits of the dead and not the voice of God or his messengers. She continues her practices despite scriptural and church teaching which condemns "spiritism" as an aberration. She preys on the grief of others, celibate and lay, to exercise her powers and fill her own coffers. Even on a human level, her helping others contact dead friends and relatives is an extreme disservice. Such contacts short-circuit the grieving process and keep people from letting go of those who have died. Further growth and healing of relationships are prevented. People need to be free to go on about their lives after someone dies. Surrendering loved ones into God's presence heals people and also brings them to new depths in their relationship with Jesus.

It is clear from Scripture and church teaching that for messages to build up the church, three things must be present: 1) the message must be doctrinally sound; 2) the charism, the messenger, and the service offered must be in submission to our pastors; and 3) the message and service must be exercised with true love for your brothers and sisters in Christ. Preying on others' hurts, financial exploitation, and the short-circuiting of the natural healing process could not be described as expressing love for others.

TO PREDICT THE FUTURE

Finally, God sometimes speaks to show you what you need to know about the future. It is important to realize that this is not the primary purpose of God speaking. Nor is it the way he speaks very often. Interpretation of such direction is difficult and conditional. Images, words, and symbols God uses to speak can be easily misunderstood and confused by human desires and anxieties. And it is always possible to be tempted and misled by the devil in understanding or responding to predictions about the future.

Consider the judgmental messages predicting the future in the Hebrew Scriptures. When the Hebrews turned from Yahweh and worshiped strange gods, the prophets warned them of the consequences of their actions. Such judgment came as a result of sin and wrongdoing. It was primarily an invitation to intimacy with God and to repentance. Predictions were always conditional, based on people's response to the message:

> Return, rebel Israel, says the LORD,
> I will not remain angry with you;
> For I am merciful, says the LORD,
> I will not continue my wrath forever.
> (Jer 3:12)

Many Catholics today are frightened by prophetic messages from the Blessed Virgin Mary at Fatima, or Medjugorje, or in Nicaragua. These messages seem to threaten a worldwide catastrophe and chastisement unless everyone is converted to God. Such predictions of disaster have been noted down through Christian history, with one consistent truth. When hearers have turned to God, the threatened punishment has been warded off. God is not in the business of beating people silly for their transgressions. The Lord would much rather see the world repent from sin and experience mercy and forgiveness.

God can also speak to help you take steps in order to prepare for the future. Certainly the angel Gabriel's message to Mary at the annunciation is a classic model of this. He named Jesus and told Mary about the mission Jesus would have so that she could have the Father's vision of her son.

So too the call and baptism of Saul of Tarsus. After his conversion and face-to-face meeting with Jesus, Saul was told, "Now get up and go into the city and you will be told what you must do" (Acts 9:6). Meanwhile Ananias of Damascus received a prophetic message and directions to go to Saul. Saul, whose name was changed to Paul, was a chosen instrument through which God would evangelize the Gentiles.

Future-oriented messages may be responded to in any number of ways. They may lead you to intercede in prayer for the people involved and the situations addressed. God can guide you toward or away from certain actions in your life. In this way you may come to a certain ministry God wants for you. Or you may simply come to a clearer understanding of a situation or opportunity that you face.

St. Frances Xavier Cabrini (USA, 1850-1917) experienced a future-oriented word from God. Even as a young girl she knew that one day she would be a foreign missionary. She was convinced also that she should go to preach the gospel to the Far East. Over many seemingly unfruitful years this prompting continued in her life. When she was finally able to establish her religious order, she went to the pope for confirmation and direction of her inner call. Yes! She was called to be a missionary, not to the East, but to the West. He sent her and her order to establish missions for the emigrants from Italy in North and South America.

During my confirmation preparation at age fifteen, I sensed that God might be calling me to become a bearer of his gospel to others. I took the confirmation name of Paul upon seeing his work in the New Testament. I forgot all about this experience during high school and most of college. In my early twenties the call renewed itself one evening while I was returning from a conference in the Midwest. I received a deep inner certitude that one day I would travel from parish to parish teaching adults how to read, pray, and study Scripture, and to reach out to others with the good news of Jesus Christ. I shared these prophetic messages with my spiritual director. He helped me enroll in graduate school to study theology, Scripture, and religious education so I would be prepared for such a ministry.

Predictive messages often have long fuses attached to them. It has taken nearly twenty-five years for these messages to come true in my life. Only in the last few years have I been involved in adult religious education and evangelization on a full-time basis. Programs and projects of the Institute that I serve in reach 2,000 - 3,000 Catholics a year, teaching people how to grow in the spiritual life, to use their charisms in ministry and to share their faith through Catholic efforts in evangelization. Hundreds of thousands of others have been touched by articles and tapes published through our office. God is faithful. The surprise is that this was not to happen in my home diocese, according to my timetable, but in God's own time and place. I have dwelt often on the words of St. Francis de Sales (France, 1567-1622), who seemed to be speaking to me personally when he wrote:

> Great opportunities to serve the Lord rarely present themselves but little ones are frequent. Whoever will be "faithful over a few things will be placed over many," says the Savior, "do all things in the name of God, and you will do all things well."
>
> I don't say that you must give up any of these good desires but say that you must bring them all forth in good order. Those that cannot be immediately put into effect should be stored away in some corner of your heart until their time comes, and meanwhile you can put into effect the ones that are mature and in season.[6]

God wants to speak to you, to give you new strength in the Holy Spirit so that you may serve others. The light of God's will can open up your mind and heart to give and to receive. The Spirit is speaking to deepen your sense of the divine presence, to encourage and console you, to guide you, to build up the church, and to predict the future. God doesn't want you to settle for anything less than the Spirit's voice in your life.

FOR REFLECTION, APPLICATION, AND DISCUSSION

Personal Reflection:

1. How has God tried to speak to you and deepen your sense of the divine presence over the past year? Try to think of two or three instances you are aware of.

2. What do you fear most about God's call to service in the church and the world? Why?

3. Fr. Solanus Casey, O.F.M. (USA, 1870-1957) suggests, "Were we only to correspond to God's graces, continually being showered down on every one of us, we would be able to pass from being great sinners one day to be great saints the next." How have you experienced this shower of grace? What keeps you from becoming a great saint?

Practical Application:

Though God may be speaking to you, you may have considerable difficulty interpreting messages. The main difficulty is struggling to know and accept orthodox teachings of Catholicism. Therefore, you may need to study your faith. One of the Catholic resources listed below would be well worth reading and rereading:

Schreck, Alan, *Basics of the Faith: A Catholic Catechism*. (Servant; Ann Arbor, MI, 1987)

Lawler, Ronald, O.F.M. and others, ed. *The Teaching of Christ*. (Our Sunday Visitor; Huntington, IN, 1983)

Sharing the Light of the Faith, National Catechetical Directory for Catholics of the United States. (United States Catholic Conference: Washington, DC, 1979)

The Catechism of the Catholic Church. (Daughters of St. Paul: Boston, MA 1994)

For Small Group Sharing or Further Reflection:

1. How have you been tempted to ignore God, or be unresponsive to the Lord's voice in everyday life?

2. Share a time when you were conscious of God manifesting a spiritual gift or charism through you to others at home, work, or in the church.

3. St. Francis de Sales (France, 1567-1622) speaks of "good desires" to serve God. "Those that cannot be immediately put into effect should be stored away in some corner of your heart until their time comes...." What are one or two of your desires to serve God that have been put into effect? Do you have any such desires stored away in your heart till they are "mature and in season"? What are they?

4. God can sometimes explain the future. How has God helped you prepare for your future? Have you ever received messages about ongoing events in your life?

5. Old Testament prophets often invited God's people back to their covenant with him. Have you ever made a covenant with God? How do you experience the need to be awakened or renewed in your relationship with Jesus?

THREE

What Can Keep You from Hearing God?

Prospect Park twittered with the voices of dozens of eager young hunters. The park director blew her whistle and off they dashed, jumping stones, lifting branches, climbing trees, even turning over trash cans in hope of capturing a bevy of hidden Easter eggs. The annual children's Easter egg hunt was off to a noisy start. Mary and Timothy, our two youngest, combed the grass and bushes meticulously, but came away with a sense of frustration. They just did not find a satisfying number of hidden eggs and chocolate bunnies.

Sometimes as an adult, you may approach hearing God's voice as if you were on an Easter egg hunt. You may dash off in all directions seeking to hear the Lord's voice. You may pry up every rock of mystical writings. You may climb the lofty heights of philosophy and psychology. You may plumb the depths of visionaries and theologians, hoping to capture a bevy of words from God. This approach can leave you with a deep frustration. Unfortunately, you may find that your hunt leaves you wandering lost in the woods of disillusionment, or worse, you stick your hand down some hole in the ground and get bitten. Perhaps you have been trapped by the occult or spiritism, or lured into a destructive cult group.

GOD THE FATHER IS VERY NEAR

Jewish and Christian tradition teaches that God the Father is very near, always speaking, and wants you to know his will. The Father is not hiding. He does not conceal his word and his will in some distant valley or galaxy, challenging you to go and find him. No, he sends Jesus, his Son, in person. Jesus is Emmanuel, God-

With-Us. The Book of Deuteronomy describes God's Word this way:

> "Nor is it across the sea, that you should say, 'Who will cross the sea to get it for us and tell us of it, that we may carry it out?' No, it is something very near to you, already in your mouths and in your hearts; you have only to carry it out."
> (Dt 30:13-14)

God has a plan and purpose for you and for the world. He loves you and invites you to love him, your neighbors, and yourself. Like a spouse or a cherished friend, the Father is eager to share himself, so that you in turn can reflect his goodness.

God's desire to communicate and reveal himself knows no limit. The prophet Ezekiel describes Yahweh as a caring shepherd, seeking out the lost, the weak, and the ill sheep. Jesus comes in the flesh as the "good shepherd" (Jn 10:1-5, 14-15) to speak to you and to guide you. The New Testament is very clear. What Christ desires is that you obey him and enter into his kingdom. Jesus is the very presence of God. He is the great "I AM" (Ex 3:14) with skin on. You can experience more than words from God.

This good news invites a response, as you turn to listen with your heart. One might venture a guess that ninety percent of what God invites you to do could be summarized in a few words from the Scriptures:

> You shall love the Lord your God with all your heart, with all your soul, with all your mind, and with all your strength.... You shall love your neighbor as yourself. (Mk 12:30-31)

One of the marks of the canonized saints in our Catholic tradition is a personal awareness of this Jesus Christ who is near and always speaking. You have but to recall the life of someone like St. Therese of Lisieux (France, 1873-1897). She often describes her "little way" into God's life. It is a sense of trust and love of the Lord to which all may aspire:

> With cheerful confidence I shall stay gazing at the sun until I die. Nothing will frighten me, neither wind nor rain. If thick clouds hide the sun and if it seems as if nothing exists beyond

the night of this life, well then, that will be a moment of perfect joy, a moment to feel complete trust and stay very still, secure in the knowledge that my adorable sun still shines behind the clouds.[1]

GOD SPEAKS THROUGH EVERYDAY LIFE

It is this sense of the continual presence of God that moves the saint to hear God's voice everywhere, through everything and everyone. When St. Maximilian Kolbe (Poland, 1894-1941) was a boy, his mother had to take him aside one day to correct his behavior. "What will become of you?" she asked. The young boy was changed by these words. He felt that God spoke to him through her. In response, he became much more obedient and prayerful.

Kolbe had the ability to hear God in the everyday things of life. Eventually this attentiveness led him to hear the Lord's invitation to offer his life for another prisoner in the death bunkers of Auschwitz during World War II. He served those around him, more aware of Jesus in them than of death.

Nor is this sense of God speaking in everyday things reserved only to the saints. I recall one of the first times I personally sensed his words to me. I was twenty-two and wondering if the path I was choosing was the right one for my life. At the time I planned to continue my studies in English literature, seeking a Ph.D. at the University of Pennsylvania. I was driving down the expressway in my hometown explaining all this to Therese, as I gave her a ride home. She then shared her plans to spend the summer working in an inner-city Roman Catholic parish, doing door-to-door evangelism. Something inside me changed. I sensed God inviting me to serve him in the same parish that summer. Just being open to God's voice that day eventually led me to give the next twenty-five years of my life to full-time lay ministry in the church.

Unlike a person on the other end of a telephone, Jesus Christ does not just give you a call. Through baptism and confirmation you are immersed in his life, words, and the power of his Spirit. The Spirit empowers you to trust that the "Sun" still shines behind the clouds of your life, and to know that God will lead you if you will follow Jesus. You can hear from God, even while driving down the expressway. You can depend on the Spirit for the strength to follow through on what you hear.

PRIDE CAN DROWN OUT GOD'S LOVE

There may be certain blocks within you to hearing God speak and to doing what the Lord wants. Before you can really be open to the Spirit's voice in your everyday life, you must deal with these. They seem to cluster around a mixture of pride and fear.

Super-spiritualism. The first block connected with pride is something called "super-spiritualism." This term means an unhealthy and dangerous overemphasis on one's personal spiritual senses in discerning God's will. Thus, it necessarily entails a blindness to how God can work through purely natural means and an unwillingness to consider the spiritual senses of others. It also implies an unhealthy absorption in what are viewed as "purely spiritual things." A super-spiritual person may seem very spiritual and knowledgeable about the ways of God, yet his or her spirituality is seriously skewed. For instance, people who appear to be holy but don't take into account natural everyday causes and leadings as possible directions from God are acting in a super-spiritual way. They seldom submit their spiritual senses humbly to others. This block characterizes many who falsely appear or claim to be mystics, saints, or visionaries.

Jill began receiving personal messages from the Blessed Virgin after her pilgrimage to Marian shrines in Europe five years ago. At first these inspirations led her to grow in fasting, prayer, the sacraments, and faithfulness to the church. This seemed to be very good. However, over the past three years she has focused too much on listening for daily messages to guide her life. Although a wife and mother of three young children, Jill spends most of her waking time absorbed in spiritual meetings, retreats, and private meditation. She refuses to listen to her pastor who has cautioned her to keep a healthy balance between the spiritual and practical aspects of her life. Jill suffers from super-spiritualism.

An aspect of her attitude originally crept into the churches from paganism. It is the belief in dualism, or a split between the spiritual world and the material world. "I will listen only to God (or one of his messengers like the Virgin Mary) and not to mere human beings. Human wisdom is evil and corrupt," says Jill. She misinterprets passages in St. Paul which mention the struggle between the spirit and the flesh (cf Gal 5:13-26). She contends that these passages mean that humanity and the world are totally corrupt and of Satan (i.e., of the flesh). Therefore they are to be avoided. Only spiritual things, leadings, and people are of any worth, she explains.

Super-spiritualism is also in evidence in her resistance to all forms of correction or input from others. Her personal spiritual experiences are absolute and right. Everyone else is wrong. In the end, what God tries to teach her through Scripture, tradition, or the church will also be seen as foreign, then irrelevant, and finally incorrect.

False Heroism. The second block of pride that can keep you from hearing God speak is "false heroism." This is the temptation to respond to God's spiritual leadings in ways that are inconsistent with your state, relationships, or duties in life. It is a sin of pride to think and act as if your service to God and the church will save the world. Jesus has already won salvation for all who turn to him, for all time. The person who expresses Christian commitment by being at the church seven days a week, at all hours of the day and night, has probably fallen into this. There are priorities of love which must be adhered to by Christians. God calls you to a quality of relationships with your family and friends as well as with members of the church. If you neglect them, they may be tempted to turn from God and the church because of your lack of love:

> Discipleship may entail heroism, but basically it signifies a willingness to go with Christ into... a life characterized not so much by great accomplishment as by humble obedience.... The Saints are not those who rise to heights of achievement, but those who sink to depths of service that most people disdain.[2]

A second aspect of false heroism is the tendency to act on spiritual promptings without reflection. You may abandon the use of reason, of thinking things through in the Spirit. The results are at best ridiculous and at worst disastrous. One night Tom was reading from the Gospel of St. Mark where Jesus called the first disciples.

He was struck by the part that said they left everything and followed the Lord. He felt that God wanted him to give away all his belongings. So, in the middle of that same night he went all over the neighborhood leaving pieces of his furniture on different neighbors' lawns. When his wife and four children woke up the next morning, they were very surprised. They were also more than annoyed at Tom. Once you abandon reason and common sense as means by which God tempers spiritual leadings and feelings, accidents and coincidences become substitutes for God's voice.

False Perfectionism. The third block involving pride that can keep you from hearing God's voice is "false perfectionism." It is an attitude implying that you already or will one day know God's will fully and completely. After that you will be perfect and in the Lord's will at every moment. You will never have to grow, stretch, or struggle again. You may become like St. Peter the apostle who wanted to set up tents after seeing Jesus transfigured:

> Perfection does not consist in doing specific things but in obeying His Will in the real circumstances of my life, not necessarily to travel to far-off lands but to love Him where He places me, not to wait for the "perfect" situation but to be with Him here and now.[3]

There is a cure for pride in all the ways it blocks you from hearing God speak. If you find that super-spiritualism is your weakness, then you are called to repent of each way that you make your own personal spiritual senses more important than God, Scripture, and the church. You also need to develop a healthy respect and humility for how God can use "natural" and everyday occurrences to show you the divine will. If you slide into false heroism, then you need to repent of abandoning the proper use of your reason and common sense when you detect a prompting from the Holy Spirit. You also need to consider in all humility whether or not you can take on an additional task at work, at home, or in your parish. And if false perfectionism is your bane, you need to repent of your desire for complete certainty. Only God has all the answers; you are only a limited creature.

FEAR CAN DROWN OUT GOD'S VOICE, TOO

The second set of blocks to hearing God cluster around fear. You can be paralyzed and kept from responding to the Lord by fear of others, fear of God, and fear of the cost of God's call. You may have only a partial experience of God's love and mercy as a result.

Out of Step with Popular Culture. Fear of others seems to have two aspects. First, you may be afraid that if you listen to God you will be out of step with popular culture and society. Fear of not being "up to date" with others can effectively block you from hearing God speak through Scripture, great spiritual masters of the past, and through the basic truths of faith. Your being "up to date with the latest" in the spiritual life must always be rooted in the best of your spiritual ancestors within the church.

A Slave to Acceptance or Rejection. A second aspect of fear of others is a slavery to their acceptance or rejection. Many in Jesus' own time would not acknowledge or follow him out of fear:

> And there was considerable murmuring about [Jesus] in the crowds. Some said, "He is a good man," [while] others said, "No; on the contrary, he misleads the crowd." Still, no one spoke openly about him because they were afraid of the Jews.
> (Jn 7:12-13)

Others became disciples, but hid their beliefs from those around them out of fear, for example — "Joseph of Arimathea, secretly a disciple of Jesus" (Jn 19:38). Finally, even the apostles struggled with this kind of fear at times. They fled when Jesus was arrested in the Garden of Gethsemane. After Jesus died they hid behind locked doors.

A man I know struggles with a similar kind of fear. Several years ago he experienced a deep conversion to the Catholic faith as a result of a death in his family. However, he is paralyzed in his response to God by fear that if he becomes Catholic, his Protestant family will disown him and never talk to him again.

Others like Sarah are afraid to admit their faith in Christ and their Catholic life to people on the job. She insists that the secular atmosphere of the business world prompts people to attack or ridicule believers. Sarah, like many, remains a frozen Christian, unable or unwilling to risk disapproval for belonging to Christ.

"Perfect Will of God" Syndrome. Fear of God is another obstacle to knowing the Lord's will. You may be afraid that God will react badly if you miss doing the divine will. The "perfect will of God syndrome" is the belief that there is one perfect will of God for your life. You must hunt and search for it, much like Easter eggs, hidden by an uncaring God.

The truth is that God wants you to know the divine will, but there are many possible ways that you might live it out. You are called to choose one of the better ones. You might compare it to a movie rating system. Four stars means that this movie is Academy Award material. One- or two-star movies may be good, too, according to the particular viewer's taste. If however, a movie gets no stars, you should save your money, because it's a definite "clunker."

There are many possible four-star "wills" of God; many ways you can please God in this life. Certainly, you want to strive to choose and live one of the better "wills," but God's primary goal is that you live in the Lord. If you strive to live the best you can, you may only have a one-, two-, or three-star will of God in your sights. The important thing is that you choose the Lord's will and not the way of sin, darkness, and Satan (no stars).

People who are caught up in this fear seem to live their lives looking backward at what might have been. They are constantly anxious and depressed. Yet God's love casts out fear.

Ralph is like this. He seems to be dragging around a ball and chain of past regrets. He once thought of being a priest, but as he was preparing to begin studies, he fell in love with Jane. He married her and now has a family. It is not possible for him to accept his marriage as God's will. He is trapped in a belief that celibate priesthood was God's perfect will for him. His wife and children are baffled by his thinking. His problem interferes with God's vision for their family.

Overly Sure of God's Will. Fear of God can be expressed by people who act overly sure of what God's will is for them. You may be afraid to admit that you don't know God's will for your life. Or you might get a small piece of it and cling to that one idea. I can own up to doing this a number of times. Once, I thought that God wanted me to live the rest of my life serving in a particular inner-city parish among the poor. It took a priest friend of mine to help me see that God might want me to love all people, rich or poor, just as Jesus did. Thank God for that insight. Much of the past fifteen years of very fruitful ministry has been among people of greater financial means, who have the same or greater spiritual needs.

Fear of Counting the Cost. Finally, you can be paralyzed by fear of the cost of this call. You may ask God for his will. You want the Lord to speak to you, but only as long as you are not asked to do something you don't like, or something that will involve suffering, for instance:

> Many people would be ready to accept suffering so long as they were not inconvenienced by it. "I wouldn't be bothered by poverty," says one, "if it didn't keep me from helping my friends, educating my children, and living respectably." "It wouldn't bother me," says another, "so long as people didn't think it was my fault." Or another would be willing to suffer evil lies told about him as long as no one believed his detractors. (St. Francis de Sales, France, 1567-1622)[4]

Your response when God seems to ask the impossible may be, "Yes, but...," or "I'll pray about that...," or "Let's wait and see...." You may be worried that God isn't paying attention to your needs. You certainly are in good company in your reluctance, as the life of St. Augustine of Hippo (North Africa, 354-430) illustrates:

> In the time before his full conversion to Christianity, Augustine had a mistress. Finally, he agreed to marry someone else.... But she was not yet the legal age, and, "I could not possibly endure the life of a celibate," Augustine writes. His mistress had left him and returned to Africa, so rather than wait for two years to be married, Augustine took a second concubine. Feeling guilty about this, he prayed, "Make me chaste, O Lord, but not yet."[5]

Fear of the cost of God's call rests in a lack of faith. Deep down you may not believe that God really loves you. You don't trust the Lord to minister to your legitimate needs. Yet God will not allow you to be destroyed, even if you die. You can endure all kinds of deaths in Jesus. He is the Resurrection and the Life. He is worthy of your trust. He is the Word and the love of God made flesh for your sake.

Part One of this book has focused on the fact that God the Father is always speaking. He does not hide his will from you. Through Jesus and in the power of the Holy Spirit the Lord offers to communicate with you daily. But you may experience blocks to hearing and doing God's will. "Super-spiritualism," "false heroism," or "false perfectionism" may afflict you. Fear of others, of God, or of the cost of the Lord's call can paralyze you. Therefore, constantly turn to Jesus in repentance and humility, seeking his healing and direction. He is faithful. Surrender to him, study to know God's will, share your spiritual journey with others and be patient (chapter one). Keep a firm hold on the purpose of God's speaking (chapter two). All these will help you overcome the obstacles to knowing the Lord's will.

FOR REFLECTION, APPLICATION, AND DISCUSSION

Personal Reflection:

1. Is searching out God's voice more like (circle one in each pair):

   a. An Easter egg hunt / mining for gold?

   b. Erecting a log cabin / building a sand castle?

   c. A clap of thunder / a whispering breeze?

Which of these images best describes your search? Why?

2. What experiences have shaped your sensitivity to God's voice? How do you feel about your ability to hear and do God's will?

3. On one side of a piece of paper write down a question or situation in your life that you would like to know God's will about. On the other side write a short paragraph describing what you suspect God's will is. Then seal the paper in an envelope and store it in a safe place until after you finish this book.

Practical Application:

Psalm 25:1-5 is the prayer of a person who has released personal preferences and hang-ups, seeking to hear and please God alone. The next time you face a situation that is uncertain, let this Scripture passage be your meditation for daily prayer. Make a decision to obey and follow God's path. Use the same meditation for several days. "Believe that you may understand the word of God." (St. Augustine of Hippo, North Africa, 354-430)[6]

For Small Group Sharing or Further Reflection:

1. Jewish and Christian tradition teaches that God is very near and always speaking to you. Share one time when you have experienced the Lord's nearness and voice in your life.

2. What is your earliest memory of hearing God's voice and experiencing divine love? How has God been present to you during a time of major decision?

3. Below are the chief blocks to knowing God's will as described in this chapter. Circle the two that influence you most.

(Pride)	(Fear)
Super-spiritualism	Fear of others
False heroism	Fear of God
False perfectionism	Fear of the cost

Why do these two blocks cripple you? How could you surrender to God's help in overcoming them?

4. God is described as the Creator of the universe, Yahweh, the Lord of Hosts, and Abba (Daddy). How do these titles help you relate to God?

5. You may have difficulty hearing from God, but the Lord has many ways of reaching you. Which imaginary instrument would help you experience God's voice better: a telegram, a phone call, a whisper, a radio transmission, a megaphone, or a hearing aid? Why?

Part Two

Ways That God Speaks in Everyday Life

FOUR

Think in the Spirit

ONE NIGHT, a father decided that his son was now old enough to go to the barn and feed the horses. The boy, however, told his father that he was afraid of the dark. The father stepped out onto the porch with the boy, lit a lantern, gave it to his son and asked him how far he could see as he held up the lantern.

"I can see halfway down the path," said the boy. The father directed his son to carry the lantern halfway down the path. When the boy reached that point, the father asked the boy how far he could see now. The boy called back to the father that he could see the gate. The father urged the boy to walk to the gate, and when the boy was at the gate, the father asked how far he could now see.

"I can see the barn," came the boy's reply. The father encouraged the boy to go to the barn and open the door. When the boy finally shouted back that he was at the barn and could see the horses, the father simply called, "Now feed the horses," and stepped into the house.[1]

God is something like the father in this story. He is with us in voice, mind, and heart. After we realize that God is always speaking, we can begin to appreciate all the forms that voice can take. In Part Two we will look at how the Lord speaks through wisdom, spiritual identity, prophetic inspirations, saints, and the church.

In this chapter we will examine human and divine wisdom as sources of God's love and personal word. By wisdom we mean the insights about how to live a better life that are gleaned from reflection on human and spiritual experience.

During frustrating moments as the parent of seven, my father would holler, "For God's sake, use your head for more than a hatrack!" Like the father in the story above, he valued human wisdom. As a creature made in his own image, God has gifted you with a mind, heart, and soul. He expects you to function through a balanced use of these gifts. Like the child in the story, you experience one of the limits of being human, when mind and emotions get all tangled up together. With the Lord's help, you must walk off into the darkness of life, trusting in what you know and searching out what lies ahead. Then God the Father will call out. He sees all the way down the path to the barn and beyond. You can walk in confidence knowing that the Lord will guide and shape the gift of human wisdom, bringing you ever more fully into the light.

UNDERSTANDING AND WISDOM

Managing your own thoughts and reviewing your human experiences is a lifelong task. In doing so, it is easy to overestimate or underestimate the value of human wisdom and thinking. One extreme involves seeing your own judgment as absolute truth. The other involves an intellectual laziness, by which you may choose to avoid thinking things through.

Ronny supervised disabled adults in a sheltered workshop (a factory designed specifically for the handicapped). When the whole program lost state funding, Ronny had no job. As weeks of unemployment dragged on, his mood swings were like blowing sand in a personal desert of his own making. He refused counseling and professional help to discover other careers. Anger and depression became guiding forces. One relationship after another crumbled. Ronny simply refused to use his own mind to deal with his problem.

Another way to underestimate the value of human wisdom is to reject thinking as unspiritual. Because the Holy Spirit can lead you beyond your own intellectual limits into the revelation of God's mind, you may view thinking as less than holy. You may be seduced into the "super-spiritualism" described in chapter three, accepting only "direct" messages as authentic. You may become frozen in anti-intellectualism, rejecting study as a valid way to experience God. Yet even when God stretches your mind with divine wisdom, the yes that you give is also an intellectual surrender. You give your mind to God, rejoicing in its limits, rejoicing in the mystery of such a gift.

The second error—of overestimating your own thinking—happens at every level of faith. It happens when a person relies on his or her own judgment without being in union with God. Good ideas become substitutes for God's will. Your ideas become law and religion for as many people as will listen and obey.

St. Bernadette's parish council spent several months discussing the needs of the church. They relied on several educated parishioners' advice, but did not refer to prayer or recent studies about the mission of the church. They concluded that outmoded buildings needed attention. The parish should build up a cash reserve to expand the rectory. This was a good idea.

Unfortunately, it did not take into account that the number of priests in the diocese would be halved in ten years, and that only 20 percent of the parish members were active. Another group in the parish sensed a call from God to evangelize in the local area, but neither the pastor nor the pastoral council would give them permission or financial help to get started. It seems that a good idea (an expanded rectory) was substituted for something that might be God's idea (evangelization).

VALUING YOUR HUMANITY

Catholic teaching offers a balance between underestimating and overestimating the value of human wisdom. It is based on an authentic assessment of the human person. Four tenets or guiding principles flow from Scripture and tradition, helping you interpret and guide what you know about yourself and others:

God created man in his image;
    in the divine image he created him;
        male and female he created them....

God looked at everything he had made, and he found it very good. (Gn 1:27, 31)

Created in God's Image. The first tenet tells you that God has created human persons, and they are very good. You are created in God's image and are somehow like God. You are filled with the breath of the Spirit, the very life of the Lord of creation. Your entire person—body, will, mind, emotions, and spirit—is "very good" in God's sight. There is a goodness to the way thoughts jump from one nerve cell to the next, echoing the Mind of minds who is, was, and ever will be.

The inspired words of Genesis are a clear invitation to value the human person. You must avoid underestimating human wisdom and thinking as inherently evil. However, focusing on this tenet alone breeds the problem of overestimating your thinking on its own terms.

Original Sin. The second tenet involves acknowledging original sin. The basic goodness of the human person is severely wounded and distorted. "...God knows well that the moment you eat of [the fruit from the tree of knowledge of good and evil] your eyes will be opened and you will be like gods who know what is good and what is bad" (Gn 3:5). Adam and Eve fell into the sin of prideful rebellion against God's will. By your participation in the human condition, you experience their sin and their fractured relationship with God and others.

Some of the great saints describe humanity in the following terms. You still possess God's image (intelligence, free will, potential to act in virtue, etc.), but you have given up the Lord's likeness (full knowledge and wisdom, intimate relationship with the Trinity, etc.). You are essentially good, but have an innate tendency toward sin:

> God is like a mother who carries her child in her arms by the edge of a precipice. While she is seeking all the time to keep him from danger, he is doing his best to get into it.[2]

St. John Vianney (France, 1786-1859) captures the situation in this poignant image. Human wisdom has been fractured and can only be completely healed by God's grace. The human mind must rely on the Lord's help to avoid the precipice. However, focusing on this tenet alone could lead to undue mistrust of your humanity and thinking.

Jesus Healed the Fracture. The third tenet focuses on Jesus, who healed the fracture between God and humanity through his birth, life, ministry, death, and resurrection. Jesus continues to restore your ability to experience knowledge and wisdom through the sending of his own Spirit. The gift of human wisdom can be revitalized as you place the Lord Jesus Christ at the center of your inner universe. Jesus died and rose for you, saving you from sin and the fallen human condition. But he also lived for you, and in his living gave your humanity its full sacred potential.

You are called to live in the light of the incarnation and the resurrection. Everyday habits based in human wisdom can be imbued with grace. When you eat right, exercise, and rest you can share in the life of Jesus:

Christ is born that by his birth he might restore our nature. He became a child, was fed, and grew that he might inaugurate the one perfect age to remain forever as he created it. He supports man that man might no longer fall. And the creatures he had formed of earth he now makes heavenly. (St. Peter Chrysologus, Italy, 406-450) [3]

Daily life becomes a doorway to the divine. The full humanity of Jesus assures you that even daily habits (that do not lead to sin) can flow with divine life. When you brush your hair, you co-create beauty and order with the Lord. When you read the daily news, you gather material for thanksgiving and intercession before God. When you work, you bring the love and presence of Jesus to all you serve.

The life of St. Philip Neri (Italy, 1515-1595) exemplified this everyday wisdom which touches the divine. Philip lived a life of joy, laughter, gentleness, and humility. In Rome he evangelized bankers, tailors, smiths, performers, barbers, booksellers, nobles, clergy, and thieves. He remarked, "A glad spirit attains to perfection more quickly than any other." Often he led his followers into the country for picnics combined with music and spiritual conferences. His down-to-earth spirituality drew many to God, though at times he struggled. "So easily did Philip slip into ecstasy that he had to read a chapter or two of his favorite joke book in order to keep his feet on the ground during Mass."[4]

Discipleship to Jesus Christ. The fourth tenet tells you that the road to a proper use of the human mind is grounded in discipleship to Jesus Christ. Through continual repentance and surrender to Jesus in daily life, you can experience the power of the Spirit. The Holy Spirit will grant God's wisdom outright or lead you through the best of human wisdom, granting you the strength to follow Jesus: "Do not conform yourself to this age but be transformed by the renewal of your mind, that you may discern what is the will of God, what is good and pleasing and perfect" (Rom 12:2).

This call to renewal of the mind was understood by St. Philip Neri also. He surrendered to Christ daily by living a simple life with few possessions. He ate meals in common with members of the groups he founded. Philip spoke of continuous repentance as a mortification and surrender of the human mind:

> They who pay a moderate attention to the mortification of their bodies and direct their main attention to mortify the will and understanding, even in matters of slightest moment, are more esteemed than those who give themselves to bodily penances.[5]

In your evaluation and use of human wisdom, always keep these four tenets in mind: 1) God has created you as very good; 2) original sin has wounded your mind; 3) Jesus comes to restore the sacred potential of your human wisdom; 4) Through daily surrender to Jesus in the power of the Spirit, you may discern divine wisdom in the best of human wisdom.

THINKING WITH GOD'S THOUGHTS

To hear God speak through both human and divine wisdom means to learn how to "think in the Spirit." You must assume an active yet yielded position before God. The desire to grasp the wisdom that God offers is crucial. An appreciation of human wisdom and this desire to understand God are treasures that Christians have inherited from their Jewish ancestors in faith. The Greek version of the Hebrew Scriptures (Septuagint—official Old Testament of the Catholic church) preserves seven books called the "writings" or "wisdom" books: Job, Psalms, Proverbs, Ecclesiastes, Song of Songs, Wisdom, and Sirach. The introduction to the wisdom books in *The New American Bible* describes the origin and purpose of these works:

The wisdom literature of the Bible is the fruit of a movement among ancient oriental people to gather, preserve and express, usually in aphoristic style [sayings], the results of human experience as an aid toward understanding and solving the problems of life. In Israel especially... The teachers of wisdom were regarded as men of God, and their books were placed beside the law and the prophets. The highest wisdom became identified with the Spirit of God.

Catholicism and Judaism share this marvelous gift of hearing the voice of the Lord behind the best of human wisdom. This understanding is the product of reflection on human experience, and the truth God has planted in the human heart.

Wisdom and Modern Sciences. The Documents of Vatican II note that the wisdom and knowledge present in the sciences of anthropology, sociology, and psychology are modern heirs to the wisdom tradition of Scripture. A challenge is presented to believers:

Methodical research in all branches of knowledge, provided it is carried out in a truly scientific manner and does not override moral laws, can never conflict with the faith, because the things of the world and the things of faith derive from the same God. The humble and persevering investigation of the secrets of nature is being led, as it were, by the hand of God, the conserver of all things, who made them what they are.[6]

Of course, these sciences are not inspired by the Spirit in the same way that Scripture is. Therefore, the church employs Scripture and tradition to evaluate and interpret the findings and conclusions of psychology, for instance. Jesus is the wisdom of God in the flesh, highlighting the best of human understanding and rejecting what is false.

Church teaching is quite clear on this point. God's revelation must judge and guide sciences like psychology, and not the other way around. Some of contemporary psychology rests on premises and tenets at odds with Scripture, tradition, and church teaching.

For example, one approach to sexual wholeness proposes sexual experiences with multiple partners of both sexes. This clearly violates Catholic moral teaching on the holiness of sex between a man and woman within marriage. When there is conflict between the wisdom of God and the world, God wins!

On the other hand, some psychological writings approach sexual wholeness as a process of accepting both feminine and masculine characteristics in each person. This theory of personal integration does not seem to violate God's revelation. Such an insight is close to the idea of the essential complementarity and unity of male and female in the Book of Genesis. A proper use of this idea may actually serve as a window on divine wisdom.

May I suggest several Catholic authors who glean truth from psychology? People like Fr. John Powell, S.J., Fr. Adrian van Kaam, C.S.Sp., and Fr. Benedict Groeschel, C.F.R., accept God's invitation to discover a Christian approach to this powerful influence in the world. You are always well-advised, however, to approach the findings of psychology and other sciences with caution, discernment, and prudence.

YIELDING YOUR MIND TO THE SPIRIT

Confront Your Thinking with God's Revelation. There are six steps which you might take if you wish to learn how to think in the Spirit. First, confront your thinking regularly with God's revelation in Scripture, tradition, and church teaching. Seek the aid of a good spiritual director or a religious educator to develop a daily plan for study. The computer field has a wise saying, "Garbage in, garbage out." If all that enters your mind and heart is incorrect or incomplete theology, then your thinking will be less than clear or wise. You need the "Bread of Life" in order to thrive intellectually, too.

Welcome God's Personal Voice in All Its Forms. Second, welcome God's voice; be open to all the ways the Lord may speak. Once upon a time, a great flood struck the Mississippi Valley. Maurice clung to the chimney on the roof of his house. As the turbulent bronze-green waters inched past the second story, he cried, "Oh God! Please help me!" A rowboat came by, but Maurice refused to let go. A Red Cross motorboat stopped. "No, thanks," he gasped. "God is going to help me." The waters churned around his waist, then his shoulders. A helicopter took one last run over the devastated neighborhood. The pilot hovered over the doomed and desperate straggler, pleading with him to grab the rope ladder. "No, thanks! I believe God is going to save me."

Finally a nearby levee collapsed and deeper, more violent waters rushed forth and drowned Maurice. He came before the Lord in heaven. "Hey, God," he complained, "how come you didn't help me when I prayed to you?" God leaned toward him and replied, "Maurice, Maurice. I sent you a rowboat, a motorboat, and a helicopter. What more did you expect?"

God's Word Overrides Conflicting Secular Conclusions. Third, let God's Word in Scripture, tradition, and church teaching override natural and secular conclusions you may feel drawn to. Rose Hawthorne Lathrop (USA, 1851-1926) was a convert to Catholicism. When alcoholism decimated her husband George, she was forced to seek a legal separation. Later her friend Emma Lazarus, who wrote the inscription on the Statue of Liberty, died of cancer. Rose was forced to face the horror and helplessness of yet another disease.

Society shunned the cancerous poor at that time. No hospital would care for them. Relatives would not take them in for fear of catching cancer. The city of New York where Rose and Emma lived consigned these people to Blackwell's Island.

Rose laid aside her natural aversion to the disfigurement and stench, and disregarded the medical opinions of the society around her. Recognizing the dignity of each human person, she insisted that these patients be treated in a warm, cheerful, homelike atmosphere with the little comforts they needed. Her work led to the establishment of the hospice movement. As Mother M. Alphonsa Lathrop, O.P., she founded the Dominican Servants of Relief who are still active in six American dioceses. She wrote:

> I will see things only through the presence of God, thus freeing myself of personality and forgetting my existence. I will regard creatures in the spirit of Jesus Christ.[7]

Take Regular Time to Think in a Prayerful Way. Fourth, take regular time to think in a prayerful way about situations you may face. Take each worry and anxiety to God, surrendering the needs, feelings, and people involved. Say, "God, you've got a problem. Show me what you want to do about it." "God commands you to pray, but he forbids you to worry" (St. John Vianney, France, 1786-1859).[8]

Take Time Away for Reflection. Fifth, take time away from the natural crush of daily events. If you want to cultivate wisdom and reflection, it is necessary to step back for a broader look. I try to take a day away for personal reflection once every three or four months. An annual retreat is something many people enjoy for the same reason.

One year I decided on a four-day private retreat. There was no special agenda or readings, other than my spiritual journal and a Bible. After a day of rest, I realized a deep loneliness within me, caused by my mother's death during the previous year. Later that day I passed a bookcase, and a volume about the reported apparitions at Medjugorje caught my eye. Reading and praying with this book reminded me of the Blessed Virgin's constant care for believers down through the centuries. I left the retreat with one consoling thought. I am not a motherless orphan as a result of my mom's death. Mary, Jesus' mother, is my mother still.

A Disciplined Thought Life. Sixth, discipline your thoughts so that you will be more sensitive to God's ways, and less likely to proceed on the basis of impulse or habit. Dom Jean-Baptiste Chautard, O.C.S.O., describes this discipline as developing "custody of the heart":

> This custody of the heart means nothing else but the habitual, or at least frequent solicitude to preserve all our acts, as we form them, from everything that might corrupt their motive or their accomplishment.... What would Jesus do; how would he act in my place? What would he advise? What does he ask of me at this moment? Such are the questions that will come spontaneously to my mind, hungry for interior life.[9]

Fr. Adrian van Kaam suggests a method for disciplining your thoughts in his book, *On Being Involved: The Rhythm of Involvement and Detachment in Human Life* (pp. 512-560). He suggests a way of stepping back from situations in order to learn how to respond as Jesus would:

A. Choose a particular reaction that is not at the Lord's disposal. For example, when you see a dirty, homeless person, is your first thought condemnation and blame, or compassion? If your first response is not, "What would Jesus do?", then you may need to discipline your mind in this kind of situation.

B. Live in relaxed vigilance with regard to your reaction and thought pattern. Catch yourself as quickly as possible when you discover such a prejudice toward another. When the next homeless person comes to your attention, be aware of your reaction, smile, and watch yourself. Notice similar reactions in other people.

C. As you grow in awareness of your reaction, make a decision to delay your usual response. Instead of immediately passing judgment, dwell on Chautard's "custody of the heart" questions: What would Jesus do? What would he advise? What does he ask of me at this moment?

D. By patient interruption of the chain of thoughts in your old reaction, you will develop a new response. Over a period of time you will find yourself thinking in the Spirit first and reacting less.

E. If you find that you have fallen into the same old pattern again, do something concrete to detach yourself from this thinking. Approach the sacrament of reconciliation or ask a friend to pray with you. Make some kind of restitution for thoughts and actions (e.g., donate to a shelter for the homeless, help out in a soup kitchen, visit a poor elderly neighbor).

By working through the six steps suggested above, you can learn how to think in the Spirit. Understanding and wisdom will become familiar pathways for the Lord's word to you. Wisdom is not an optional gift for scholars or saints, but a foundation for everyday spiritual life. Understanding readies you to be an active, yet yielded disciple of Jesus:

> If you can't obey in little things, it is impossible to obey a Gospel that is contrary to all common sense and logic. God's ways are above ours. Whatever he asks is always absurd by the standards of human wisdom.[10]

FOR REFLECTION, APPLICATION, AND DISCUSSION

Personal Reflection:

1. Which of the two errors in assessing human wisdom are you more prone toward? (check one)
    ___ underestimating human wisdom
    ___ overestimating human wisdom
Why do you suppose this happens?

2. Which one of the tenets of Catholic teaching about the human person is most significant in your life? What are some reasons for your choice?

    a. God creates human persons as good.

    b. Humanity is distorted through original sin.

    c. Jesus restores and redeems the human person.

    d. Discipleship and surrender to God bring life.

3. Describe an occasion in your life when you received wisdom from the Holy Spirit. Describe a time when you experienced common sense as a gift from God. How were these situations similar and different?

Practical Application:

Fr. van Kaam describes a process for disciplining your thoughts and practicing "custody of the heart." Choose an area of your thinking that is not at God's disposal. Try applying this approach over the next three weeks. If you like, keep notes in your spiritual journal about what happens, or discuss your results with a spiritual director or confessor.

A. Choose one reaction not at God's disposal.

B. Keep relaxed vigilance for times when this happens.

C. Delay your usual reaction; ask yourself what Jesus would do.

D. Patiently interrupt the mental and emotional chain of thinking as often as possible.

E. Use confession, penance, and restitution to help separate yourself from your actions, and to learn a new way of thinking.

For Small Group Sharing or Further Reflection:

1. Some Christians reject the human mind and wisdom as unspiritual. What would be the Catholic response to such an attitude? Why?

2. What is your favorite passage from the wisdom books of the Bible (e.g., Job, Psalms, Proverbs, Wisdom, Song of Songs)? What message do you get from this passage?

3. What does it mean to think in a prayerful way about a situation or person? What is your experience with doing so?

4. "We should attain the same level of education in our faith as we have in our secular lives." Do you agree or disagree? Has study of your own faith matched the level of your schooling? What educational needs do you have? How do you feel about the availability of adult religious education in your parish?

5. Which of the six steps to "thinking in the Spirit" are most difficult for you? Why?

   a. Confront your thinking with God's revelation.

   b. Welcome God's personal voice in all its forms.

   c. Let God's Word override conflicting secular conclusions.

   d. Take regular time to think in a prayerful way.

   e. Step back from daily life for reflection.

   f. Discipline your thoughts.

FIVE

Discover Your Spiritual Identity

S HE HAD A BURNING DESIRE to imitate the apostles as they gathered in the cenacle, or upper room, to await the outpouring of the Holy Spirit on Pentecost. While other teenage girls went to parties or settled down to raise a family, she gave herself a theological education, sneaking away to read her brother's books. He was studying for the priesthood. By age nineteen, Blessed Elena Guerra (Italy, 1835-1914) had such a sense of her own identity before God that she launched out to care for the victims of cholera around her hometown of Lucca. Soon over five hundred joined her in this apostolate. With a few friends from this group, in 1872 she began the Oblate Sisters of the Holy Spirit.

Her spiritual identity was so enmeshed with a call to follow the Spirit that she wrote twelve confidential letters to Pope Leo XIII between 1895 and 1903, urging intense devotion to the Holy Spirit for the entire church. In response Pope Leo published an encyclical about the Spirit called *Divinum Illud Munus*. He also began the year 1900 and the century by singing the "Come, Holy Spirit" in the name of the whole church. Elena was the first person beatified by Pope John XXIII, and therefore an inspiration in his prayer for a new Pentecost while preparing for Vatican Council II. Blessed Elena yearned,

> Oh, if ever the "Come, Holy Spirit" which, since the Cenacle and after, the Church has not ceased repeating, could become as popular as the "Hail Mary!"[1]

The same Spirit of God is also within you, forming your self-image and identity in the light of God's love, ready to help you experience the delicate balance of mature self-love without self-indulgence. A Christian man or woman needs a healthy self-awareness, a sense of "This is who I am!" A self-awareness provided by God becomes raw material for discerning the sources of spiritual leadings:

> For this reason it is essential to spiritual discernment that we be in touch with our feelings.... Many people say it is very difficult to know God, since we do not see him, hear him, or touch him as we do another human being. This is true, of course, but I have become convinced that the greatest obstacle to real discernment (and to genuine growth in prayer) is not the intangible nature of God, but... our own lack of self-knowledge—even our unwillingness to know ourselves as we truly are. [2]

As you come before God you will discover who you really are, much as Elena did. God has made you unique. You are irreplaceable. You are a blend of talents, needs, genes, emotions, intellect, and soul. You are a reflection of your Father-God. You may not yet appreciate how God speaks through your own spiritual identity, but God will delight in revealing it to you. He knows you better than you know yourself, and with more patience.

When our son Peter was preparing for his First Communion, he had a lot of questions. How could Jesus come to him in a personal way, and to all the others in the church as well without somehow being diluted or diminished? None of our explanations satisfied Peter. Finally we took him to Fr. Jim, who had the perfect answer for our curious son. "Jesus is like a very large mirror reflecting God to us. When we break the mirror into hundreds of pieces, then look down, we still see the same whole picture, Jesus."

You can hope to be like that mirror reflecting Jesus, no matter what shape, size, age, or personality you are. Let the Lord guide you in a search to uncover your particular call and mission in his sight. Scripture also refers to God as the potter who shapes you and then makes use of your gifts in a unique way. Let the Lord mold your self-image.

For me it has sometimes been a struggle to see myself with the Lord's vision. For many years I did not even like to look in a mirror because of my large frame and build. More than one doctor has tried to help me lose weight without success. Perhaps what has been most helpful is God's patient love in prayer and the support of my Christian brothers and sisters.

Over several years, God has zeroed in on one talent, one emotion, one commitment at a time, until slowly Jesus has revealed the whole picture of who I am as his brother. For example, my abilities to analyze, plan, and administrate were reinforced as God's gift through an invitation to become a parish director of religious education, and through my wife's willingness to play strategy games like "Risk."

Zero in on some areas of your inner life in order to discover your own spiritual identity: first, your gifts and talents; second, needs and emotions; third, the ministry and commitments you have; and finally, your style of spirituality.

THERE'S GOLD IN YOUR BACK YARD

Jesus tells the parable of the talents which are gold, silver, or copper coins (Mt 25:14-30). Each of three servants was given money to take care of. It was not unusual for one servant to bury such a treasure in the backyard for safety's sake. But the whole point of the story is that your gifts and abilities are just that, given. There is a wider purpose for your ability to drive a car or read a book. Gifts small and large will bring great fruit when used for the Lord. God will speak to you about how to spend them.

Part of your struggle may be discovering the gifts you have. It may take some work to identify them, or some consultation with others. You might ask yourself what you are good at. I enjoyed writing poems and composing religious folk songs as a young person. Even though I am not involved in a music ministry now, people still ask me to sing and play guitar. They experience healing, even though I know only the bare essentials about the guitar, and must ask others to transcribe my songs onto paper after I compose them.

St. Ambrose (Italy, 340-397) was the just and learned governor of two provinces. He went to Milan to help settle a bitter dispute between two factions over who would be elected bishop there. As the story goes, someone shouted out, "Ambrose for bishop!" and poor Ambrose was unanimously chosen. He protested so vehemently that he was put under house arrest, until eight days later when the Emperor made it official. Ambrose was baptized and then consecrated bishop on the same day. He threw himself into learning all he could about God, and put his incredible political talents to use in building the church in the whole of Western Europe. Even though he did not choose God, when chosen, he surrendered his gifts:

> When we speak about wisdom, we are speaking of Christ. When we speak about virtue, we are speaking of Christ. When we are speaking about justice, we are speaking of Christ.... When we are speaking about truth and life and redemption, we are speaking of Christ.[3]

You might also discover your gifts by looking harder at what you think are only faults and shortcomings. When I am at a Christian gathering, I get upset if no one is reaching out to stragglers and people who are alone. This points out a gift for drawing people into a group. My daughter Mary sometimes nags us when we haven't eaten out at a restaurant for a long time. Nagging certainly isn't an appropriate way to get what you want, but this kind of attentiveness shows that Mary has a gift for recognizing the social needs of our family. You may find that what could be your strongest gifts get you in the most trouble. When redirected toward God, though, they will bear fruit.

RECOGNIZING FEELINGS AND NEEDS AS TOOLS

St. John Vianney (France, 1786-1859) is an example of coping with some very basic feelings in discovering who you are in God. Some individuals in the huge crowds that came for confession were so foul-smelling that he used a small bottle of vinegar to revive himself. Still each one felt loved. His reputation for holiness was so great that souvenir-seekers would snatch bits of his hair, clothing, and even the mortar from his cottage. Yet he coped with patience and humor. When one woman asked for a saint's relic, he replied, "Go home and make your own!" On another occasion jealous priests in the diocese circulated a letter saying that he had no background for giving spiritual direction. When the letter reached him by mistake, he signed it too.[4]

It is part of the human condition to experience feelings and needs, and to respond to needs and feelings around you. The marvel of St. John Vianney is that his sanctity and humanity shone through in his patience and good humor, even in very trying circumstances that would have frustrated, perhaps even embittered, many others. Emotions are a movement from within, telling you that something is happening. They are morally neutral, but can be responded to in holy or sinful ways. Anger points out a discrepancy between what you see and want. Jesus reacted with righteous anger when he drove the moneychangers out of the temple precincts. Fear shows you something more powerful than you. It is important to listen to feelings, search out the needs they identify, and respond in ways that give life to you and others. The key point is that emotions can be helpful signals and reference points for inner life. It is important to evaluate strong emotions before taking drastic action.

At one time I was working over forty-five hours a week administering a large parish religious education program. We also had three small children. It was hard for me to relax after work, and even harder after helping Therese get the children settled for the night. I took my need for relaxation to God. A quote from St. Theresa of Avila (Spain, 1515-1582) struck me, "Heaven preserve me from sullen saints."[5] That's just what I was becoming. I thought about childhood hobbies that I had laid aside, and decided to start reading super hero comic books again. It was a blow to my "adult" pride, but I enjoyed myself and felt recreated by God as I spent time reading them.

It is important to voice your needs before the Lord. Then lay them at the feet of Jesus and walk away:

> "Do not worry and say, 'What are we to eat?' or 'What are we to drink?' or 'What are we to wear?' All these things the pagans seek. Your heavenly Father knows that you need them all. But seek first the kingdom [of God] and his righteousness, and all these things will be given you besides." (Mt 6:31-33)

What you really need will be given back, and even become a source of God's leading in your life. A need for friends becomes a call to community. A need for money points out a chance to reorder finances in God's presence. It is only when you look at a need without God, that trouble arises. St. Thomas Aquinas (Italy, 1225-1274) said, "No one can live without delight, and that is why a man deprived of spiritual joy goes over to carnal pleasure." [6]

As you surrender your desires to God, the Spirit will make room for Jesus in your heart. The clutter of so many needs will give way to a longing for union with the Trinity which is your most consuming need. St. Gregory the Great (Italy, 540-604) describes this passion for God. He is the pope who fostered the Gregorian chant in liturgical worship. The music itself speaks of great emotion channeled into disciplined melody:

> For it is not our words that make the strongest impression on the ears of God, but our desires. Thus, if we seek eternal life with the mouth, but not really desire it with the heart, when we cry out we are silent. But if we desire in the heart when our mouth is silent, in our silence we cry aloud... and the voice is heard in secret when it cries out in silence with holy desire. [7]

USING PSYCHOLOGY TO SORT THROUGH NEEDS AND EMOTIONS

Christianity employs many tools to help you get in touch with yourself in a healthy way that is not overly introspective. Prayer, study, sacraments, service, teaching, retreats, journals, and examination of conscience are some of the more noted ones. God has also given you the science of psychology (the study of the mind and of human nature). If properly used it can reveal much, especially in the area of needs and emotions that benefit from God's healing light. Vatican Council II notes:

> Let the faithful incorporate the findings of new sciences and teachings and the understanding of the most recent discoveries with Christian morality and thought, so that their practice of religion and their moral behavior may keep abreast of their

acquaintance with science and of the relentless progress of technology: in this way they will succeed in evaluating and interpreting everything with an authentically Christian sense of values. [8]

Christians can study the observations of science and look carefully at the values and philosophies behind different theories. For example, one view of secular psychology holds that people are self-creators of their universe, having the final say in their own happiness. This, of course, is opposed to the belief that God creates, and it is therefore incorrect. However, the grain of truth involved is that it takes a personal decision to live for God's goodness and the sake of others. Christians believe that God made the first decision and is the source of happiness, wholeness, and personality.

The church proposes a balanced view of psychology. You can consider its insights without necessarily sliding into the idolatry of certain schools which glamorize introspection, pleasure, or self. Humans are not totally independent beings. The human person is good but distorted. You need Jesus, who is "the Way."

For the Christian the center of life and self is Jesus Christ, the glorified Son of God. A life of faith colors and gives meaning to needs and emotions. The "Burger King" theory of human personality, "Have it your way," self-destructs. Jesus is THE Way, THE Truth, THE Life. At the same time, following Jesus as the way brings you into a paradox. You are called to love and yet deny self. On the one hand, Jesus commends the scribe who believes the great commandment to love the Lord and your neighbor as yourself. On the other hand, Jesus warns his disciples about self-centeredness:

> "Whoever wishes to come after me must deny himself, take up his cross, and follow me. For whoever wishes to save his life will lose it, but whoever loses his life for my sake and that of the gospel will save it." (Mk 8:34-35)

The apparent paradox is resolved if you recall God's purpose in creating humanity. You are very good yet fallen in nature. Let God reveal and develop that basic goodness. Also let God minister to your fallen or warped needs and emotions, even if it means surgery.

THE IMPORTANCE OF LEARNING TRUST

One insight from psychology that has helped me is from the realm of child development. The point is that infants first learn trust from their parents. Religious educators would also add that parents are the first models of God for the young child. Therefore, to trust a parent's love eventually helps you trust God as well as others. At first you imagine God to be a big parent. This is normal. Unfortunately, this also means that problems between parent and child will often mean broken faith in God.

When I was born, my mother almost died from phlebitis and clots in her legs. One leg developed an uncontrollable ulcer. She was confined to bed, and I was shuffled back and forth to a neighbor. At about five months old, I reacted to Mom as if she were the stranger, so my parents took me home for good. Then for many months I suffered from several respiratory infections that meant treatment in the hospital pediatrics ward. I was there so many times that the nurses kept photos of "their" baby over the counter at the nurse's station.

God has helped me face issues of trust and mistrust that probably go all the way back to that time. This awareness has given me patience with myself. I've also experienced inner healing of mistrust through prayer and reception of the sacraments.

Beverly suffered from a fear of men and also of God. Because her earthly father had been a violent alcoholic, she could not relate to men, or even to God if he was described in masculine terms. She realized that her problem stemmed from childhood experiences and sought professional help in counseling. When I met her she had been in therapy for some time with little progress. She attended a course about daily Scripture prayer. As Beverly read and prayed with passages about God's love, she found the father she never had. The Lord gave her an inner assurance of her deceased father's love as well. When this happened, her counseling began to move forward:

> Just as Christians are susceptible to colds, broken bones, and various diseases requiring medical attention, they are susceptible to mental problems, repressions, and various psychologi-

cal difficulties such as phobias, obsessions, depressions and the rest.... Various psychological applications have helped many, including committed Christians. [9]

God's mercy can touch you with healing as you uncover deeper needs. Fleeing from the self-knowledge that the spiritual life offers can lead to psychological sickness. Purification from old wounds is essential if you hope to have clarity about God's will. Use the tool of professional help if you need it. But be careful to choose someone with values close to those conveyed in the good news of the gospels.

LOOK AT YOUR COMMITMENTS AND YOU MAY RECOGNIZE YOUR CALL TO MINISTRY

Another way to experience God's hand in your spiritual identity is to look at the commitments you have made. How have you already decided to spend your talents? What direction have you already taken in meeting your own needs and those around you? Even though past decisions were not necessarily made with the eyes of faith, the events and commitments you face today are God-given opportunities to serve Jesus.

Shirley attended a talk about Christian marriage. She had a beautiful new relationship with God, but was disgruntled about her husband's lack of faith. She asked a question, bemoaning her very "unchristian" marriage. The speaker turned and replied, "Don't you think that God knew you even when you didn't know him? Isn't it possible that he picked Paul for you, knowing what would happen?"

Some commitments may need re-examination, but it is safe to say that most will become ministry as you bring an awareness of God's call into the workaday world. Often, my commitments as a father have given me a clear indication of God's will for me. At certain times it has been important to change jobs in order to be faithful to providing for my family. At other times it has meant learning how to discipline a toddler or teach a teenager how to drive.

St. Frances of Rome (Italy, 1384-1440) is a model of following God through personal commitments. She was married to a nobleman and in love with Jesus, all at the same time. Daily prayer and sacrifices came before wealth and position. Loving her family was

God's will for her despite her desire to live as a religious. When Frances was sixteen her faith led her to defy the normal pattern for mothering as a noblewoman. She decided to nurse her own baby son, Giovanni, and raise him herself. Her own words can inspire you no matter what your occupation or gender:

> It is laudable in a married woman to be devout, but she must never forget that she has a household to care for, and sometimes she must leave God at the altar to find him in her housekeeping.[10]

In his book, *Driven by the Spirit: The Life of St. Frances of Rome with Reflections,* Daniel F. Stramara, O.S.B., Oliv., explains:

> Although she was a simple woman, Frances knew how to live the ordinary and transform it into the extraordinary....[Her] life teaches us that holiness is accepting ourselves as we are, while striving to become all that we can be in God and for God. (p. i)

DEVELOPING YOUR OWN STYLE OF SPIRITUALITY

As you read the lives of the saints, you may notice that they were people who knew their spiritual identities. Part of this identity surfaced in each saint's unique style of spirituality. A devotion to the Holy Spirit marked the spirituality of Blessed Elena Guerra (Italy, 1833-1914). Surrender to God colored that of St. Ambrose (Italy, 340-397). St. John Vianney (France, 1786-1859) had a certain wry sense of humor in relationships with God and others. St. Frances of Rome (Italy, 1384-1440) saw loving family as a key to living for the Lord.

My own spiritual identity is tied up with the cross of Christ. His suffering and the paradox of life springing from death echo deep in my being. Time and again I am called to relive the death and resurrection of Jesus, especially through the sacrifices of full-time lay ministry and through our family's chronic allergies.

You, too, have a particular call or stance before God. It is rooted in the source of all Christian spiritualities — the life/death/resurrection of Jesus and the coming of the Spirit — the Paschal mystery. It is the flowering forth in your life of your baptism, confirmation and Eucharist.

One way to discover your style is to look at the religious and scriptural symbols or events that touch you most deeply. How do they speak to you of the Lord Jesus? How do they reveal the Father's love for you and aspects of who you are before him? How do they tap into the power of the Holy Spirit?

My wife is drawn to the Lord of creation and to Jesus as the incarnate Word of God. Some other possibilities include: being a child of God, living the Word and gospel, being saved by Jesus the redeemer, or being a devoted child of Mary. Many religious orders are formed around a distinct spirituality, devotion, or rule originally lived out as a part of the spiritual style of the founder:

> When the truth shines in a soul, and the soul sees itself in the truth, there is nothing brighter than that light or more impressive than that testimony.... Shining out like rays upon the body, it makes it a mirror of itself so that its beauty appears in a man's every action, his speech, his looks, his movements, and his smile.[11]

Today's challenge and excitement is searching out your spiritual identity, or patiently letting one develop over time as God speaks to you in different ways. Some people learn about themselves through experiences with other Christians. The focus provided by renewal movements and small faith-sharing groups resounds like a bell rung in the depths of their hearts and spirits. Many in the charismatic renewal have chosen a devotion to the Spirit of God, for example. People who have experienced Marriage Encounter have chosen their sacramental union in Jesus as a focus of spirituality. One couple in our parish always receives the Eucharist side by side, as a sign of their identity before God.

Bring all of your talents, needs, emotions, and commitments into your relationship with the Lord. Let that relationship color all the rest. In our society all too often physical identity is what takes top billing. Young and handsome or slim and beautiful is important. Inner life is considered secondary. For the Christian the opposite is true. Who you are before God is meant to color everything else about you and give overall direction to your life. God has called you and given you particular talents that make you unique. Your spiritual identity is an important way that the Lord wants to speak to you.

FOR REFLECTION, APPLICATION, AND DISCUSSION

Personal Reflection:

1. List five gifts and talents that you have. List your greatest shortcomings. How are they related to one another?

2. How do current commitments make use of your gifts and talents? How do you experience yourself as being spent for others, or for God, through these commitments?

3. What favorite scriptural image or symbol might give you a clue to your spiritual stance before God? Why?

Practical Application:

Match the saint with his or her leisure activity.

1. __ Therese of Lisieux	a. jokes and riddles
2. __ Thomas More	b. keeping a travel diary
3. __ Catherine of Siena	c. oil painting
4. __ Frances Cabrini	d. care for stray animals
5. __ Philip Neri	e. a pet monkey
6. __ Francis of Assisi	f. cooking for friends
7. __ Theresa of Avila	g. dancing to castanets

Sometimes leisure choices point out hidden talents. Which saint would you have had the most fun socializing with? What are your three favorite leisure activities? What do you like most about each one? How does each one bring you closer to or farther away from God? (Quiz answers are in note 12 for this chapter.)

For Small Group Sharing or Further Reflection:

1. Self-awareness can provide much of the raw material for discerning which spiritual leadings are really from God, and which are primarily from your own desires. How does this statement coincide or disagree with your experience?

2. Do you find psychology to be a gift or a tool for personal and spiritual growth? Why or why not?

3. God answers you. How has God helped you with specific needs or desires? What needs has he asked you to surrender?

4. What feelings are you most comfortable sharing with others or with God? How do you express feelings as part of prayer?

5. Among holy people you have known or read about, whose style of spirituality is most like your own? Why?

SIX

Are the Days of Prophecy Gone?

Yes, days are coming, says the Lord GOD,
  when I will send famine upon the land:
Not a famine of bread, or thirst for water,
  but for hearing the word of the LORD.
Then shall they wander from sea to sea
  and rove from the north to the east
In search of the word of the LORD,
  but they shall not find it. (Am 8:11-12)

ARE THESE WARNINGS from the prophet Amos meant for us today, or just for the Israelites over two thousand years ago? Some believe that the time of prophetic inspiration ended with the Hebrew prophets or with the death of the last apostle. Are the days of prophecy gone for you?

A Gallup poll entitled "Beliefs about Ways God Speaks to People" was conducted in 1986 for the Christian Broadcasting Network. Over two-thirds of the one thousand thirteen Americans in this scientific sample claimed to hear from God through prophetic inspirations. Thirty-six percent believed God speaks to them directly, 39 percent through other people, 48 percent through internal feelings and impressions, and 49 percent through the Bible.[1] Applying these percentages to the Roman Catholic population of our country indicates that as many as forty-six million active and inactive members of our church may hear from God regularly.

It seems that God is very busy speaking to us. God, in fact, is always speaking to all who will listen. The problem is largely that we place limits on how and when we expect God to speak. We may be limited in our awareness of the many ways the Lord speaks. We may not recognize the common forms of inspiration from God. This chapter will consider four forms of prophetic inspiration: interior senses, exhortation, direct messages and signs. Then we will look at how we can more fully yield to these inspirations today, much as the prophets and apostles did.

INTERIOR SENSES

You may expect something like a mystical cloud, or thunder and lightning to accompany God's voice. Though such experiences may have enthralled Moses, Peter, and some of the notable saints, even in the Hebrew Scriptures God often speaks through more ordinary means.

After Elijah the prophet put the prophets of Baal to death, Ahab and Jezebel (king and queen of Israel) tried to put him to death. Elijah fled to a cave in the wilderness of Horeb and waited for God to speak. First he experienced a heavy wind; then an earthquake. But God did not speak through either one. Then came a fire. Still no sign of God:

> After the fire there was a tiny whispering sound. When he heard this, Elijah hid his face in his cloak and went and stood at the entrance of the cave. A voice said to him, "Elijah, why are you here?" (1 Kgs 19:12-13)

Elijah experienced God's voice in a tiny whispering sound. It was so natural as to go almost unnoticed. But he had ears to hear. God can also speak to you in very ordinary ways. One possibility is the experience of interior senses from God. It can be so subtle as to be mistaken for good thoughts. But these are thoughts, intuitions, and echoes of conscience which have been gently formed by the movement of God's Spirit. As you grow in the Christian life these touches of the Spirit bubble up from a well of inspired common sense within. They are true prophetic messages from God.

David was a young adult teaching a seventh-grade religion class in the parish where I was director of religious education. Every week he dropped into my office with lots of questions about

God, the church, and Scripture. As we spoke together one week, a thought danced across my mind. I should ask him how things were at home. I waited a moment, then followed this inspiration. Tears came to David's eyes as he poured out the painful story of a broken relationship with his mother. That interior sense was a key in ministering to David.

St. Ophelia's Parish Home and School Association gathered quarterly to help support the Catholic elementary school. The spring meeting had just opened when the chairperson read a message. The Bradley family home had burned down earlier that evening. This parish family with four children had lost all their belongings. The chairperson stopped the meeting. Based on an inner sense of God's leading, she did two things: first, she led us in prayer for the fire victims; then she invited us to establish a special fund for the family. A sense of peace and hope settled on those gathered. We felt led to start the collection right then and there.

EXHORTATION

A second form of prophetic inspiration is exhortation. This is a word spoken by others in a way that revives, renews, and strengthens you in your life with the Lord. At times it can be a challenge or admonishment, bringing about a new direction in your life with God. Simple suggestions when received in God's Spirit can become exhortations.

Jesus exhorts the disciples many times in the New Testament. One day they were out on the lake when a very severe storm approached. They were panic-stricken and awakened Jesus for help. He calmed the wind and then asked them why they had no faith. His question challenged them to trust the Father on much deeper levels than ever before. You can imagine that you are an apostle as you read Scripture, and let Jesus exhort you. He wants to empower you to follow him.

While a high school student, my wife Therese heard the testimony of Sister Karen Miller who worked with the poor in New York City. Sister Karen often ran short of funds for her soup kitchen and begged for money to help feed the hungry. One day she approached a very well-dressed businessman on a street corner to ask for help. The man sneered at her with contempt and spit on her. She replied, "Thank you! That was for me. Now what can you give to Jesus and his poor people?" The man repented on the spot and gave very generously. Her words were an exhortation that challenged this man to grow. Her telling of the story was an exhortation to Therese, challenging her to consider ministry in the church as part of her own vocation.

DIRECT MESSAGES

Direct messages are a third form of prophetic inspiration from God. The warning from the prophet Amos at the beginning of the chapter is an example. These messages may come through dreams, visions, apparitions, locutions (voices from within or from outside of you), through certain words or thoughts. In Scripture, lives of the saints, and many spiritual writers, these are the most prominent channels of inspiration. This section will describe each kind of direct message and give examples. Later chapters will examine how to know which direct messages are from God and how to interpret and apply authentic inspirations to your daily life.

Dreams. Dreams have a long history as channels of God's voice for people of faith. In Scripture the stories of two Josephs are important examples. Genesis 37-50 recounts the life of Joseph, son of Jacob. He dreams that his brothers will one day come and bow down before him. They become irate and sell him into slavery in Egypt. Later Joseph lands in jail over another misunderstanding and is freed because of his ability to interpret dreams. This gift eventually brings him into leadership in Egypt under the Pharaoh.

When famine strikes Canaan, Joseph's brothers must go to Egypt seeking food. A marvelous reconciliation takes place after the brothers are humble and contrite enough to bow down before Joseph.

Joseph, son of Jacob, in St. Matthew's Gospel is betrothed to Mary. But she becomes pregnant before they live together. After Joseph decides to divorce Mary, rather than exercise his right to have her stoned, God speaks to him in a dream:

"Joseph, son of David, do not be afraid to take Mary your wife into your home. For it is through the holy Spirit that this child has been conceived in her.... When Joseph awoke, he did as the angel of the Lord had commanded him.... (Mt 1:20, 24)

St. John Bosco (Italy, 1815-1888) received many prophetic messages through dreams. In 1876, St. Dominic Savio, a former student of John's, appeared to him in a dream:

> Dominic himself was beautiful and glorious, and he appeared in the company of many other blessed souls [Dominic had died in 1857]. He gave Don Bosco three slips of paper; in one the priest saw the faces of [his students] who were living in their baptismal innocence. In the second he saw those who had fallen but were trying to rise from their sin. When he opened the third paper [boys living in mortal sin] it gave off such a disgusting and nauseating stench that Don Bosco abruptly awoke; he found that the disgusting odor still clung to his clothes.[2]

Visions. Visions are interior pictures and may have accompanying words that form in the mind conveying a message from God. A person receiving a vision may be awake or in a trance. In a religious trance, there is an intense mental concentration. Consciousness may be lost altogether, or consciousness may remain while voluntary movement is lost.

On St. Paul's second missionary journey, he was kept from entering the province of Asia to preach the gospel. Finally, they arrived at Troas on the northwest coast of modern Turkey. Paul had a vision of a Macedonian asking for his help. He left at once to preach the good news there (Acts 16:9-10). This vision and Paul's response were especially significant because they led to the establishment of the first Christian community in Europe.

A young woman I met in 1970 was deeply involved in the Catholic charismatic renewal movement at Holy Cross College, Worcester, Massachusetts. She periodically attended Mass with her mother at St. John's Parish in inner-city Worcester. As she prayed one morning after Mass, she received a vision of the church filled with over one thousand people singing and praising God in a charismatic manner. She felt led to go to the pastor of the parish and ask to start a weekly Catholic charismatic prayer meeting in the church. The group started slowly in the late 1970s, yet she eventually saw her vision fulfilled. Masses celebrated by St. John's prayer group grew from twenty-five people to over a thousand each week. As she rejoiced, this young woman recognized a face from her 1970 vision among the priests who concelebrated the liturgy.

Apparitions. Apparitions are a kind of vision appearing outside of the person who sees them. They may therefore be seen by more than one person at the same time. The appearance of Moses and Elijah at the transfiguration of Jesus seems to have been an apparition:

> After six days Jesus took Peter, James, and John and led them up a high mountain apart by themselves. And he was transfigured before them.... Then Elijah appeared to them along with Moses, and they were conversing with Jesus. (Mk 9:2, 4)

In the past four hundred fifty years, the most famous appari-

---

WHAT ARE THE APPROVED MARIAN APPARITIONS?

Although nearly 80,000 apparitions of Mary have been claimed since the third century A.D., only seven have been officially approved (but not made obligatory) for private devotion by members of the Catholic Church, according to Fr. Johann Roten, director of the International Marian Research Institute, University of Dayton, Ohio. Such approval means that the apparition involves nothing contrary to faith and morals and that it highlights some aspect of public revelation (Scripture, Tradition and the Teaching Office of the Church). These are:

1531, Guadalupe, Mexico: On a hill outside Mexico City, the Blessed Mother appeared four times to a recent convert to Christianity, Juan Diego. Mary proclaimed herself "the Mother of the true God who gives life" and left her image permanently upon Diego's "tilma" or mantle.

1830, Paris, France: In the chapel of the Daughters of Charity of St. Vincent de Paul, Mary showed herself three times to novice Catherine Labouré (age 24). She was commissioned by the Virgin to have the medal of the Immaculate Conception or "Miraculous Medal" made in order to spread devotion to Our Lady.

1846, La Salette, France: Six thousand feet up in the French Alps, Mary came to Maximin Giraud (age 11) and Melanie Calvat (age 14) while they

tions have been those reported about the Blessed Virgin Mary. She has appeared to individuals and groups giving strong prophetic messages for the world from her Son, Jesus Christ. In 1531, Mary appeared in Mexico to Blessed Juan Diego, a poor peasant. Her apparitions as Our Lady of Guadalupe led to the conversion of over eight million Indians to Christianity. Since her appearance in France in 1858 to Bernadette Soubirous, thousands have been healed and converted to Jesus by visiting the shrine of Lourdes. When Mary appeared to three young children at Fatima, Portugal in 1917, over one hundred thousand people witnessed the sun dancing in the sky at midday.

These Marian apparitions, which have been recognized as authentic by the church, all seem to have similar characteristics. Mary appears to simple, poor people. Graces of the Holy Spirit are experienced by those present, including repentance, conversion, joy, gifts of prayer, and peace. Healings and miracles often occur among people who make pilgrimages to the site in the months and years following.

---

tended sheep. Her appearance in sorrow and tears called for conversion and penance for sins.

1858, Lourdes, France: At the Grotto of Massabielle, the Virgin showed herself eighteen times to Bernadette Soubirous (age 14). Under the title, "the Immaculate Conception," she called for penance and prayer for the conversion of sinners.

1917, Fatima, Portugal: While tending sheep, Lucia de Santos (age 10) and her two cousins, Francisco (age 9) and Jacinta Marto (age 7), experienced six apparitions of Mary, who identified herself as "Our Lady of the Rosary." Mary urged prayer of the Rosary, penance for the conversion of sinners and consecration of Russia to her Immaculate Heart.

1932-33, Beauraing, Belgium: Mary came thirty-three times to the playground of a convent school to five children (ages 9-15), Andree and Gilberte Degeimbre, and Albert, Fernande and Gilberte Voisin. Identifying herself as "the Immaculate Virgin" and "Mother of God, Queen of Heaven," she called for prayer for the conversion of sinners.

1933, Banneux, Belgium: In a garden behind her family's cottage, the Blessed Mother appeared to Mariette Beco (age 11) eight times. Calling herself the "Virgin of the Poor," Mary promised to intercede for the poor, the sick and the suffering.

Chapters eleven and twelve will discuss discernment and our response to such things as Marian apparitions and prophecies.

Locutions. Locutions are voices from God or one of God's heavenly messengers that speak from inside or outside your body. They may come with no other spiritual manifestations. God's call to Samuel the prophet in the Hebrew Scriptures seems to have been a locution. "When Samuel went to sleep in his place, the Lord came and revealed his presence, calling out as before, 'Samuel, Samuel!' Samuel answered, 'Speak, for your servant is listening'" (1 Sm 3:9-10). Though St. Paul both saw and heard Jesus at his conversion on the road to Damascus, "the men who were traveling with him stood speechless, for they heard the voice but could see no one" (Acts 9:7). They experienced a locution.

St. Teresa of Avila (Spain, 1515-1582) is one of the church's authorities on locutions. Teresa was often guided by locutions in reforming her religious order, the Carmelites. She describes the experience of receiving such a gift:

> The divine locution is a voice so clear, that not a syllable of its utterance is lost. It may occur, too, when the understanding and the soul are so troubled and distracted that they cannot form one sentence correctly: and yet grand sentences, perfectly arranged, such as the soul in its most recollected state never could have formed, are uttered.[3]

Words and Thoughts. St. Thomas Aquinas (Italy, 1225-1274) remarks that "grace builds on nature." It should be no surprise that one of the most common ways that God gives direct messages is in cooperation with human words and thoughts. God's Spirit within may bring messages and ideas to mind which can easily be put into words (some spiritual writers call these "intellectual locutions" — the messages without an audible voice). You recognize God's words in this and feel the urge to put the message in the first person singular. With deepened sensitivity and experience, you can discern the weight of God behind this experience. Sometimes you just get an image, a few words, or a phrase which repeats itself in your mind.

You may feel an urge to begin speaking aloud or to write down the message that comes. It may be helpful to record the essence of this message in a spiritual journal. Such messages should be reflected upon and submitted to your spiritual director, pastor and/or mature Christian friends before any important decisions are made or acted upon.

Messages and prophecies like these have often been used by God to call individuals and the church to repentance. St. Catherine of Siena (Italy, 1347-1380) is a powerful example of proper reception of and ministry with such prophetic messages. She was called by God to help purify the church of her time. The Lord spoke through her with such authority that she even became an advisor to the pope. St. Catherine is recognized as one of the Doctors of the Church in the spiritual life. Through her God has called many to holiness. Consider one such message:

> By Adam's sinful disobedience the road was broken up so that no one could reach everlasting life.... [and] there came the flood of a stormy river that beat against [you] constantly with its waves.... But I wanted to undo these great troubles of yours. So I gave you a bridge, my Son, so that you could cross over the river, the stormy sea of this darksome life, without being drowned.[4]

Some months ago, I had a very threatening nightmare. It happened a few days before a speaking engagement. All the fears and anxieties I have ever imagined about public speaking lashed out at me. I awoke in a bath of sweat with the feeling that, as a Christian, I was totally inadequate and "hopelessly flawed." I have experienced things like this at times from the evil one before speaking and writing, so I simply turned a little more intently toward the Lord and put the feelings aside. During my final prayer before speaking, the words that formed in my mind gave me great consolation and inspiration. It seemed as if God was saying, "You have been afraid that you are 'hopelessly flawed,' but from this day on I call you to be 'flawlessly hopeful.'"

People attending Catholic charismatic prayer meetings today may hear such messages spoken aloud while in worship. Usually during the praise and prayer portion of the meeting, several people receive words and thoughts accompanied by an urge to speak these to the gathering. Each person takes some time to pray for purification of the message before speaking and waits for the proper time in the meeting to speak. Then, with love for all there gathered, the person speaks his or her message aloud to the group, preceded by a convention such as, "My children" or "My people." Such conventions are helpful to alert the group that this seems to be a prophetic message from God. After the message is delivered, the whole group is led by the worship leader to reflect, weigh the content, and apply the message to their own lives. Afterward the person who spoke out approaches a few of the group's leaders to discuss the value of the message he or she spoke.

SIGNS

Signs are a fourth form of prophetic inspiration. They are concrete persons, places, things, or events that show us the presence and power of God. The lives of some of the Hebrew prophets were in themselves signs. Amos was a simple shepherd sent to remind people of God's care. Hosea was married to a prostitute. Her unfaithfulness illustrated the relationship between God and the northern kingdom of Israel.

Healing, exorcism, and miracles comprise the major signs of God's activity in the Scriptures. "Many signs and wonders were done among the people at the hands of the apostles" (Acts 5:12; cf. 2:43). Christian mysticism and the lives of the saints expand the list of possible signs to include spiritual smells, touches, tastes, sounds, music, and the weather. Anti-Catholic groups in nineteenth-century Italy attempted to beat and shoot St. John Bosco (Italy, 1815-1888) several times. Then one night as Don Bosco visited the sick, a large gray dog joined him, shielding him. Many times "Grigio" (Don Bosco's nickname for the mastiff) joined the saint in his nocturnal rounds. The dog appeared and disappeared mysteriously as a personal sign of God's care and protection of St. John Bosco.

Alice evangelizes people in an unusual way. She perceives a spiritual glow or shadow over the faces of people she meets. She first started to see this sign over individuals returning from Communion at Sunday Mass. When someone with their face in shadow came by she felt urged to go and talk to the person afterwards. Since she began to reach out this way, she has led scores of people to a closer relationship with God.

Thousands of people today have attended Catholic charismatic healing services. One particular sign gift occurring at these services is sometimes referred to as "slaying" or "resting" in the Spirit. People line up to present themselves for a time of personal prayer with the leaders of the service. As a gesture of unity and blessing, the priest or lay people involved place their hands on the head or shoulders of each person. Then they spend some time in prayer over the person.

Suddenly that person may fall over backwards onto the floor without being hurt and lie there for some time. If God's Spirit has prompted the falling phenomenon, some healing or grace or significant call from God may come as he or she lies there bathed in God's grace.

The Need to Be Cautious with Signs. Several difficulties with signs make them unreliable as a single source of divine guidance. They can be misunderstood, misinterpreted, and misused. Jesus performed signs and wonders that astounded those who followed him. Yet some Jewish leaders imagined he was using these gifts to gain political power. Jesus debriefed the seventy-two disciples returning from their mission of preaching and healing. He had to caution them; "Nevertheless, do not rejoice because the spirits are subject to you, but rejoice because your names are written in heaven" (Lk 10:20). You must seek first the God of signs and wonders, not the signs and wonders of God.

Signs from God can be misinterpreted. The Jews thought that Jesus' grave was empty because his disciples had stolen his body (Mt 28:11-15); whereas the empty tomb heralded the resurrection of Jesus to believers. The cross of Jesus was a sign of triumph over suffering and death. But to the Romans of Jesus' time, execution by crucifixion was the lowest form of degradation reserved for common criminals.

When have you made a deal with God? "Lord, I'll go back to church if you heal my sister, mother, wife, or child. Lord, I'll help out in the parish religious education program if you get the pastor on a Cursillo, Marriage Encounter, or into a Life in the Spirit Seminar... or on a pilgrimage to my favorite Marian shrine." Asking God to guide your every step through supernatural intervention smacks of prideful presumption and manipulation.

You must ask yourself why you ask for signs from God. Is it because you are unaware of the myriad ways God already speaks to you? Is it because you wish to avoid making decisions? Is it because you refuse to heed the messages God has already given? Are you trying to control or manipulate God or others? If the answer to any of these questions is yes, then you need to repent of your attitudes and actions. You need God to show you how to start over again in seeking his will.

YIELDING TO SPECIFIC INSPIRATIONS

God wants to fill you with inspirations. How can you empty yourself to receive these? Below are eight concrete approaches you can use to make yourself available for God's messages. The list is not totally inclusive.

First, learn to listen and wait upon the Lord. Unless you choose to develop a daily prayer life it will be more difficult for you to hear God clearly. In my own experience of prayer, fifteen to twenty minutes is the bare minimum. During your prayer time commit yourself totally to the Lord. Clear your mind by offering up distractions one by one to God, so you can rest in his presence.

Second, keeping a journal helps make you sensitive to God. Simply get a notebook and begin. Each day during your prayer time write a short letter to Jesus about how things are going in your life. Explain how you feel and are dealing with a particular problem or struggle in your life. End it and sign it just like a letter to a friend. Then be very quiet and imagine Jesus sitting down to write a short letter to you in response. Write as if Jesus were speaking directly to you. This dialogue will slowly become more like a conversation with Jesus Christ as you get used to it.

Third, pray with Scripture. Several resources at the end of this book will give you help to do this well. See also the related resources by the author.

Fourth, listen to Christian music and relax in God's presence for a while. Toward the end, record thoughts, impressions, and inspirations that come to you.

Fifth, use aspirative prayer to enter into God's presence. This is a peaceful repetition of prayers like, "Lord Jesus Christ, have mercy on me, a sinner," or "I love you, God," or even just "Jesus," as you breathe slowly in and out. Beginners may find it helpful to do this twice daily for fifteen to twenty minutes, in order to establish the habit.

Sixth, learn how to do spiritual reading. Read a good spiritual book slowly. Listen for God to speak. Record striking words and images from the book in your spiritual journal. Review what you've written periodically. Books by Susan Muto listed in the bibliography may help.

Seventh, become comfortable with silence. Take either a few hours or a whole day once a month to rest in silence. An annual quiet retreat could be scheduled. It's hard to hear God speak if there is no silence in your life.

Eighth, learn how to fast and sacrifice. Loosing the bonds of appetite for food and material things will help make you available for spiritual food and the things of the Lord.

PRIVATE REVELATION

All of the ways God speaks to individuals today (since the death of the last apostles) are part of what our Catholic heritage calls "private revelation." Catholic theology makes a clear distinction between these and "public revelation," which includes the life and teaching of Jesus, Scripture, tradition, and church doctrine. Private revelation must always be submitted to the judgment of public revelation. Even if found to be authentic, private messages from God can never have as much authority as, or add to, revelation already given us through Scripture, tradition, and the teaching office of the church.

Catholics are not required to believe any private revelations, even if they are declared authentic, because they are not part of doctrine. For instance, even though the church has declared them to be authentic, Catholics are not required to believe in the Marian apparitions of Fatima, Lourdes, and Guadalupe. Catholics are encouraged to consider prophetic messages or genuine private revelations if they find them helpful in their spiritual lives.

This chapter has described four forms of private revelation through prophetic inspirations: interior senses, exhortation, direct messages, and signs. Our purpose has been primarily to open you up to a new outpouring of spiritual messages. We bypassed the entire problem of determining whether a particular inspiration is authentic or false. That will be dealt with in Part Three, "Living a Life Open to God's Voice" and Part Four, "Responding to What God Says."

FOR REFLECTION, APPLICATION, AND DISCUSSION

Personal Reflection:

1. Think of examples of interior senses, exhortation, direct messages, and signs from the Bible, especially in the New Testament. What form of prophetic inspiration do you think God used most often to speak to people during biblical times?

2. Circle below the form of specific inspiration from God that you have experienced. Indicate how often.

    a. Interior Senses   c. Direct Messages

    b. Exhortation   d. Signs

Why do you suppose God chooses to speak to you in this way? How comfortable do you feel with the other forms of inspiration?

3. What could you do to increase your sensitivity to prophetic inspiration?

Practical Application:

Praying Scripture is a key approach to receiving God's prophetic inspirations. Try the daily method below for a month and then review what you hear God saying with your spiritual director, pastor or a mature Christian friend:

1. Choose a passage in which God speaks to someone (Maybe the "Book of Consolation" in Isaiah the prophet would be a good starting place — Isaiah 40-66 — or the first letter of John.) Pray and ask the Holy Spirit to speak.

2. Begin reading the passage, listening and allowing the words to evoke feelings. Try to break your reading up into five-to-ten-verse chunks, stopping when you come to a natural break in the thoughts expressed.

3. Go back and read your five to ten verses again. Circle or underline words, phrases, thoughts, or images that strike you (i.e., trigger a positive or negative reaction).

4. Choose one of the verses you marked and write it down in your spiritual journal under today's date. Include the book, chapter, and verse it came from.

5. Paraphrase the verse underneath in your own words as if God is speaking directly to you about your life.

Example

Scripture Verse: "Comfort, give comfort to my people." (Is 40:1)

Paraphrase: "John, listen to your wife. Help her with the loss of Rachel as she goes away to college."

6. If an inspiration comes, allow the message to continue as if it were a letter from the Lord to you.

Example:

"You know that I love Therese and Rachel more than you do. Help Therese to appreciate the fine young woman your mutual love has nurtured. Send her forth with that same love."

NOTE: Don't be concerned if it feels artificial or awkward as you write God's word to you. As you try this method, trust God to use your thoughts and words to speak. God is with you. God's love is incarnate.

For Small Group Sharing or Further Reflection:

1. How has God given prophetic inspirations to a friend, relative, or favorite saint of yours? How well did that person respond?

2. Share a time when you have experienced a prophetic inspiration (interior sense, exhortation, direct message, or sign) from God. How has this inspiration affected your life or decisions you've made?

3. What is the difference between "private revelation" and "public revelation"? How does this distinction cause you peace or turmoil as you struggle to hear God speak?

4. Who is your favorite prophet in the Bible? How did that person hear God's voice? Are there similarities between the struggles this prophet faced and those in your own life?

5. God can speak through a mixture of words and images. Which of the two are you most comfortable with? How could you grow in appreciation for God's visual revelations?

SEVEN

Saints: Highway Signs to God's Way

IT WAS EARLY OCTOBER and we were planning a series of family liturgies at St. John's Parish. Children's class time, music, and the format for worship had been decided. The question that we struggled with the most was whether to move into the main body of the church, or celebrate Mass in the "All Saints Chapel" downstairs.

As we discussed our needs, it became evident that there was a strong attachment to the smaller chapel. Many felt a kinship with all the unknown saints. There were hundreds of people just like us enjoying the presence of Jesus in heaven. They stood like highway signs along the Christian way of life, pointing toward God's voice.

We decided to have family liturgies in the chapel, and celebrated our decision by planning an "All Hallow's Eve" party. Each of us dressed up like a favorite saint, instead of like a Halloween character.

I chose St. Martin de Porres (Peru, 1579-1639), an intriguing character from one of our children's storybooks. He was born the illegitimate son of a Spaniard and a Panamanian woman. According to legend, he once rid a monastery of mice by inviting the tiny animals to another building where he would feed them daily. But mouse taming was perhaps the least of his talents. Not even his abilities in bilocation and aerial flight compared with his ministry to the poor and homeless. He cared for the poor, the sick, and the hungry in Lima, even ministering to African slaves chained in Spanish galleys. He also led the rich into a concern for the African slaves. His example challenged me to welcome disheveled inner-city parishioners to our family liturgies and into my life. Pope John XXIII canonized him in 1962 as a patron of interracial justice. Through Martin, God was speaking to me about social justice.

If you had been invited to our "All Hallow's Eve" party, what saint or living Christian would you have chosen to imitate? Would you have chosen Martin for his gift of social justice, so relevant to our own disjointed American society? What saint's life in this book or elsewhere has challenged you?

Jesus gives a description of people like St. Martin in Luke's Gospel. A large crowd was gathered around Jesus and it was impossible for his relatives to reach him:

> He was told, "Your mother and your brothers are standing outside and they wish to see you." He said to them in reply, "My mother and my brothers are those who hear the word of God and act on it."(Lk 8:20-21)

Saints are those who hear the word of God and act on it. They live out a desire to do the Father's will as he reveals it to them. They hope to know Jesus as closely as his own family did.

Your favorite saints and spiritual heroes are road signs pointing toward God's call for you, and toward your own spiritual identity. The church is made up of a multitude of people who have followed Jesus down through the centuries. They come with all manner of personalities and talents, walking ahead of you and beside you. In this communion of saints you have the opportunity to stop and meet them as part of your daily Christian journey. They can be a rich source of prophetic inspiration and spiritual encouragement.

John Henry Newman was very different from St. Martin. He was a brilliant Anglican theologian (England, 1801-1890). His passion for understanding God eventually led him to follow Jesus into Roman Catholicism. Newman never again enjoyed the recognition and productivity that he left behind for Jesus' sake when entering the Catholic church. Still he continued to respond to Jesus through gifts of scholarship and administration:

> Everyone who breathes, high and low, educated and ignorant, young and old, man and woman has a mission.... [God] deigns to need every one of us... not to get what we can out of [life]

for ourselves, but to labor for him. (Cardinal John Henry Newman, England, 1801-1890) [1]

When I was a teenager I wanted to go to dances. There was one problem. I couldn't dance. So I asked my older sister Claire to teach me. That was a disaster. My overabundance of left feet and tantrums were unbearable. So I watched American Bandstand on television and slowly perfected one step after another.

The church has a process that watches a person's whole life for steps in the dance of faith. It is called canonization. Those who have survived this discernment process are models for the universal church community. If you pay attention to them, you are presented with a portrait of discipleship that will help you hear God's voice too. If you develop a relationship with some, you will grow with them.

CONFESSORS, MARTYRS, SERVANTS

What do the saints have to say to you? They speak to you and draw you close to God as confessors of the faith, martyrs for the faith, and servants of the Lord. Some are known as confessors because they defended the faith against strong anti-gospel values. St. John the Evangelist (Galilee, c. 6-104) is a confessor. Another example is St. John Chrysostom (Syria, 347-407) who preached and taught to correct the abuses of heresy in the fourth century. St. Catherine of Siena (Italy, 1347-1380) worked and wrote to resolve a controversy over who the legitimate pope was in the fourteenth century.

Other saints are notable for lives that came to a climax in martyrdom. Edith Stein (1891-1942) was a German Jewess who became a cloistered nun in 1934. Her own search for truth was sparked by watching a widowed friend's serenity during her husband's funeral, and by reading the autobiography of St. Teresa of Avila. As Hitler's strength grew in Germany, Edith did not consider escape to be her first priority. When arrested she rejoiced. "Come," she said to her sister, "let us go for our people." [2] She was put to death in Auschwitz in August, 1942, and is being considered for canonization.

Others who gave witness by shedding their blood include: St.

Stephen (Judah, d. c. 35), St. Joan of Arc (France, 1412-1431), and St. Ignatius of Antioch (Syria, d. c. 102) who was an elderly bishop, and all but one of the apostles. The martyr's desire to give every breath in an act of worship is expressed by St. John Brebeuf (France/Canada, 1593-1649), a Jesuit missionary to the North American Indians in the 1600s:

> I vow to you, Jesus my Savior, that as far as I have the strength I will never fail to accept the grace of martyrdom.... Here and now I offer my body and blood and life. May I die only for you.... In this way, my God and Savior, I will take from your hand the cup of your suffering and call on your name: Jesus. Jesus. Jesus. [3]

Catholics also rejoice in those who have responded to Jesus through a variety of ministries as servants of the Lord. The possibilities are endless. Many have molded their personal discipleship around vows of poverty, chastity, and obedience, like St. Therese of Lisieux (France, 1873-1897), St. Elizabeth Ann Seton (USA, 1774-1821), or Blessed Damien the Leper (Hawaii, 1840-1889). Others had gifts in the area of teaching, healing, or administration.

I appreciate the humor of St. Vincent de Paul (France, 1580-1660) as he spearheaded a whole movement dedicated to serving the poor. Naive benefactors would sometimes offer impractical or disorganized clothing. St. Vincent's response to one woman who gave unpaired shoes was, "You would be surprised how few people there are with one foot."[4]

There have also been saints with extraordinary charisms like St. Teresa of Avila (Spain, 1515-1582) who experienced visions and locutions, or St. John Vianney (France, 1786-1859) who could read people's hearts. Crowds flocked to him for confession for over twelve hours a day. These two saints responded to inspirations with great humility. Neither was prone to be overly serious, always guarding against pride.

Catholics have not always known how to respond to such gifts. St. Joseph of Cupertino (Italy, 1603-1663) is a humorous example. Miracles were so common in his life that his superiors kept moving him from one monastery to another to avoid mobs of pilgrims. Eye-witnesses report that he experienced levitation at least seventy times. One perhaps befuddled response of the church to the charism has been to name him the patron of air travel and pilots.

The church's vision of the saints also includes holy women and men who are Old Testament examples of friendship with God. They responded to Yahweh according to the gifts of faith that were possible before the time of Jesus:

> What more shall I say? I have not time to tell of Gideon, Barak, Samson, Jephthah, of David and Samuel and the prophets, who by faith conquered kingdoms, did what was righteous.... Therefore, since we are surrounded by so great a cloud of witnesses, let us rid ourselves of every burden and sin that clings to us and persevere in running the race that lies before us while keeping our eyes fixed on Jesus....
> (Heb 11:32-33; 12:1-2)

These people don't get to wear a big letter "S" on their shirts, but then neither do you, or your friends and relatives who have gone before you as disciples of Jesus. There are Saints and saints. You have known holy men and women, unrecognized by the church or society, but filled with a humble goodness that touched you, making you aware of the kingdom of God. Listen to them, as they too invite you to hear God's voice.

COMMUNION OF SAINTS

The road to holiness is traveled by all who die in Christ, the great cloud of saints described in the heavenly vision of the Book of Revelation (Rv 7:9-17). They are people who live ordinary lives in an extraordinary way. The church celebrates them on November 1, the Feast of All Saints. If you could see them as individuals, most would be anonymous strangers from every corner of history and civilization.

You might also recognize the familiar face of a loved one or friend. I would notice Juan Correa, a fellow college student of mine. He studied chemistry hoping to return to his homeland of Colombia to teach. He had unusual gifts of love and humility that brought many into our college faith-sharing group. As graduation approached, he confessed strong fears about the political and personal dangers that Christians faced in Bogota. Still, his love for his people drew him there like a magnet. Just two years later Juan contracted polio. As he lay paralyzed and dying in an iron lung, his one wish was to listen to Scripture all day. Within weeks of his death, two of his sisters who were experiencing high-risk pregnancies were healed.

I would also recognize Jeannia Young, my wife's grandmother. She had gifts of faith and prayer that have sustained all of us. Jeannia lived the last thirteen of her ninety years in a nursing home. Her daily routine included a trip down the hall to pray the rosary in the chapel and to "visit the poor old people who have nobody." Even if it took hours with a walker, that didn't matter.

Noontime Mass on television was also important to her. She was willing to skip lunch for Mass when a new schedule was instituted. "First things first," she would explain. Finally the nurses gave in and served her in her room after Mass. Fr. Dolan challenged us at her funeral by asking, "When you are old like Jeannia, how important will it be to have a chapel nearby? How important will it be to love Jesus and to pray each day?"

YOU ARE A SAINT

You are also included in the communion of saints. You have been washed in the waters of baptism and drawn into the body of Christ. You are called to hear God's word and act on it, becoming either a confessor, martyr, servant, or friend of the Lord. You are called to live prophetic inspirations with humility and obedience. You can examine your life for signs of discipleship in order to repent when you don't find them and rejoice in God's mercy when you do. Sainthood is a gift:

> Put on then, as God's chosen ones, holy and beloved, heartfelt compassion, kindness, humility, gentleness, and patience, bearing with one another.... And over all these put on love.... (Col 3:12-14)

In another sense, you are not yet a saint. While you still live on the earth you have the option of turning toward or away from God. Even a person like Mother Teresa of Calcutta stands before

Jesus every day with this same incredible choice. Perhaps this is why you feel a little uneasy when you are addressed as a saint. You are only too aware of your dependence on the power of the Spirit to say yes.

In the fifth century the church formalized the Apostles' Creed, which avows belief in the communion of saints. This statement has a prophetic tone for our day. Modern culture places a high priority on being active, young, and future-oriented. Managing automobiles, electronic equipment and timetables are commonplace skills. Unfortunately this means people are tempted to devalue the past, contemplation and old age. The only thing more irrelevant than being old is being dead. The church speaks out in contrast to this prejudice, connecting saints of the past, present and future.

Oneness in Christ is not interrupted by death. Believers are all in the same boat with Jesus. The old *Baltimore Catechism* called living believers the "Church Militant" (struggling through life's choices on earth), and believers who have died, the "Church Triumphant" (glorified and enthroned with Christ in heaven). Together all believers make up the mystical Body of Christ. This fellowship pulsates with the life of Jesus, who is the center and fulfillment of all time past and present. You can look backward and forward knowing that he will come again, drawing you into eternal worship together with all the Saints and the saints with a small "s":

> In the lives of those who shared our humanity and yet were transformed into especially successful images of Christ... God vividly manifests His presence and His face.... Our companionship with the saints joins us to Christ, from whom as from their fountain and head issues every grace and the life of God's people itself.[5]

SAINTS: HIGHWAY SIGNS TO GOD'S WILL

What help can dead people, however holy, be to you? First, the saints can inspire you through their example to draw close to God. They are both models of discipleship and teachers that you can rely on. I find myself being attracted to St. Ignatius of Loyola (Spain, 1491-1556), a strong-willed soldier who liked to be right.

God first got his attention after a serious leg injury and lengthy convalescence. Following Jesus always meant surrender for Ignatius, constant surrender of his own will. I find myself being led in the same way. So do many other Christians:

> We should never have prodigies of conversion and marvelous holiness if they had not changed the flames of human passion into volcanos of immense love of God. (St. Frances Xavier Cabrini, USA, 1850-1917)[6]

Second, the saints can help when you turn to them with your needs. In a real sense, you can talk to the saints the way you would to a friend. They live now, forever, in the Lord's presence. They are intercessors for the living, placing you before the Lord. St. Therese of Lisieux (France, 1873-1897), wrote, "I want to spend my heaven doing good on earth."[7] So she has. Claire and Harry asked her daily intercession during World War II. They promised God that if Harry returned safely from fighting in the Pacific, they would name their first daughter Therese. And so they did.

I would not hesitate to ask a dear friend to pray for me. I can do the same with the saints, relying on their union with Jesus. I like to compare talking to a saint during prayer to a conference call. As I share my feelings with St. Joan of Arc (France, 1411-1431) or St. Bonaventure (Italy, 1221-1274) there is someone else on the extension excited about greeting me. Jesus is listening and waiting for me to finish. When I stop talking to one friend, the natural thing to do is turn to the other friend, Jesus, who is always present.

There have been countless times when people have hung up before speaking with him. These occasions are usually only indications of a need for deeper conversion and healing. This is especially true when asking for the intercession of a loved one who has recently died. At such times you might also benefit from an equal amount of small group sharing time with living saints, like family and friends. Remember, both parts of the church are a source of God's word for us, those saints in heaven and on earth.

Third, a saint's life is a sign of the kingdom, something like a highway sign. One of the dangers of living in a fast-moving, highly organized world is that there is too much information about too many saints, especially if you have ever picked up *Butler's Lives of the Saints* in four unabridged volumes. You may be tempted to ignore them. Perhaps you are like drivers on Route 95 through the Bronx, New York. Many of the highway signs are obliterated with graffiti, making a safe journey for the uninitiated almost impossible. So too with what you see about the saints. You must make an effort to understand what each one has to say to you, to ensure a better understanding of God's will.

MAKING FRIENDS WITH THE SAINTS

There are many ways to choose a few saints as special friends for your Christian journey. You wouldn't want to be friends with hundreds of them. You can't do that with earthly people. But a small community that you can call on from time to time is helpful. You might read through a calendar or dictionary to acquaint yourself with "your new neighborhood," so to speak.

When I first began meeting the saints in my "spiritual neighborhood," I started with St. John the Baptist (Judea, c. 3 B.C.-A.D. 28), a namesake. Jesus called John a prophet. St. Mark quotes Isaiah in describing John,

"Behold, I am sending my messenger ahead of you;
he will prepare your way." (Mk 1:2)

This call to be a messenger of God was something that rang true in my life also. I have responded to this call by helping thousands of Catholics to meet the Lord through praying and studying the Scriptures alone and in groups. John the Baptist helped me hear this call and to persevere.

Native-born American saints like St. Elizabeth Seton (USA, 1774-1821) have also had an impact on my spiritual life. She is easy for me relate to, as a married person from the northeastern United States. She dealt with family illness and worked at combining ministry with parenting. Her example has strengthened me in my own acceptance of chronic illness. Elizabeth also served the church as a Catholic educator and gave witness to the communion of American believers extending through our history as a nation. She wrote,

What was the first rule of our dear Savior's life? You know it was to do his Father's will. Well, then, the first end I propose in our daily work is to do the will of God. Secondly, do it in the manner he willed, and finally, do it because it is his will. [8]

As you listen to a saint with your heart, God will touch you. This happens whenever God speaks, but is usually more defined when you meet a flesh-and-blood model of faith. The words, actions, and events in the saint's life call forth a personal response. You are either attracted or repelled by that saint's desires, values, or actions. You are inspired and challenged by the saint's example.

SEEK OUT WHAT ATTRACTS AND WHAT REPELS YOU

When you identify with a saint there is a surge of grace. You can flow with the Spirit in a new way. The Father touches a nerve, a spot where he can work. God invites you to respond to him in a way that is similar. People attracted to Pope John XXIII (Italy, 1881-1963), for instance, are warmed by his combination of simplicity and courage. They long to imitate him in a complex world.

There was a time when I could not read something about the life of Mother Teresa of Calcutta without crying. My spiritual director helped me see how God was calling me to new levels of compassion and holiness. It was a time to yield.

There are also saints who trigger something very different in you. You do not immediately experience the promise of living water bubbling up inside. Instead there is a churning and an unrest. You feel like fighting what a particular saint represents. You may be repelled by certain qualities on first acquaintance.

St. Francis of Assisi (Italy, 1181-1226) is likable when you picture him with baby animals, but what about when he begged for money in the street? What about St. Stephen (Judea, d. c. 35) who forgave his executioners? You may find it hard to forgive a driver who cuts you off without signaling, much less a thief or a murderer. Yet this resistance can also be a fruitful opportunity to experience God's voice and touch.

Your response can indicate the call to an "opposite" gift. Suppose you are the parent of five children. St. Francis' embrace of abject poverty may repel you. His shoeless, unwashed, unkempt condition does not fit with your state in life. Your duty to create a healthy home environment does not match his call and is confirmed by contrast.

At other times, unattractive qualities may point out your unmet needs, attachments, and sinfulness. The resistance you feel may well be at the cutting edge of grace and repentance. Denise was uncomfortable with the story of St. Stephen's martyrdom when she read it on Sunday. She knew persecution and suffering from the inside. Denise was a young widow and an adult child of two alcoholics. Her teenage son, Jack, had physically abused her, robbed her, and run away from home a few months earlier.

She had been struggling with forgiveness and fear for quite a while. In response to St. Stephen's story, and other leadings from God, she turned from her own overwhelming feelings and went to look for Jack. She found him in an abandoned building and told him that she loved and forgave him. A few short weeks later, Jack was stabbed in a fight with a drug addict. As he lay dying in a hospital emergency room, he was reconciled to God through the ministry of a passing priest. Denise's forgiveness had helped bring her son into the Father's arms.

Lay people may be repelled by most canonized saints at first glance. It may seem that only priests and religious are offered as examples of holiness. As a single or married person, it is hard to relate to these people. Most are also from a different time and culture.

The key to a new appreciation of the saints is not to be absorbed by the differences, but to look for similarities. Consider saints whose professions are the same as yours. Note the qualities that you admire and befriend a saint on that basis. The communion of saints is like your extended family. You have some relatives with whom you experience many bonds. Other relatives share only a common ancestor. You accept them all in some way as family. So, too, with the saints who are your brothers and sisters in Jesus Christ. If some are unattractive, ask the Lord to clarify your response and his will for you.

Finally, certain qualities have been recognized in all the saints by spiritual writers: a willingness to give and reveal self, faith, simplicity, and a willingness to grow. Embrace these qualities in your own life and you will find yourself on the path to sainthood, a path shared by spiritual friends extending through time and space.

Saints stand like highway signs, pointing out possible responses to the Lord as confessors, martyrs, servants, and friends. All the baptized are called and claimed to be saints too.

We can profit from the example of those who are like older brothers and sisters in faith, asking their prayers, learning about ourselves through what attracts and repels us in their journeys with Jesus.

FOR REFLECTION, APPLICATION, AND DISCUSSION

Personal Reflection:

1. Name three holy men or women—everyday saints—whose lives have had an impact on yours. Why did you choose each of them?

2. What three canonized saints do you feel closest to? What is it about each of them that attracts you?

3. Name three holy people whose lives or words have challenged you the most. What do you think God might be saying through them about conversion, healing, or faith?

Practical Application:

Perhaps you would like to meet a saint, or reacquaint yourself with an old friend in Jesus. A dictionary of saints, calendar, or collection of biographies might help you make a selection. Try one of those below:

Ball, Ann, *Modern Saints: Their Lives and Faces, Vols. I & II* (TAN Books: Rockford, IL, 1983, 1990).

Cruz, Joan Carroll, *Secular Saints* (TAN Books: Rockford, IL, 1989).

Delaney, John J., *Dictionary of the Saints* (Doubleday: Garden City, NY, 1980).

Newland, Mary Reed, *The Saint Book* (Crossroads: New York, 1979).

After you select a saint, you may want to read a biography to learn more about him or her. Some saints have also written works themselves. When reading a biography, select a writer who presents the saint's faith and struggles in a realistic way. When reading a saint's work, keep his or her time period in mind, in order to appreciate the context of what is said.

For Small Group Sharing or Further Reflection:

1. Saints "hear the word of God and act on it" (Lk 8:21). How could you follow this advice more closely?

2. Four kinds of saints were described in this chapter: confessors, martyrs, servants, and friends of God. Imagine that it is the year 2100, and a future pope has just canonized you. If this seems far-fetched, imagine yourself in the multitude of saints described in the Book of Revelation. Aren't you hoping to join them someday? Which of these four categories would you fit into? Why?

3. What do you think about the practice of praying to the saints in heaven? Has it been helpful in your life?

4. Name the person who has had the most profound spiritual impact on your life. What has touched you most deeply about his or her life?

5. Consider the life of Jesus Christ. What attracts you most? What repels you? What might the Lord be saying to you through these experiences?

EIGHT

Hear God Speak Through the Church

THE MEETING TO PLAN an interdenominational retreat on knowing God's will suddenly screeched to a halt. An argument exploded about the ways God speaks to people today. Martha, a friend from a biblical fundamentalist church, exhorted, "Scripture is the way that God speaks today!"

"But God also uses the gifts of the Holy Spirit to lead people," countered George, a denominational Pentecostal.

Helen, a Greek Orthodox woman, insisted, "we must not forget how God speaks through tradition in the church."

"No! No! You are all wrong," bellowed Mel, a Roman Catholic. "God only speaks today through the pope, bishops, and pastors!"

From a truly Catholic understanding, each of these views is correct and yet incomplete. All of the ways God speaks are important. What's critical is that we hear the Lord together where and when we need guidance and live accordingly. At the same time, we need help to interpret the messages that God speaks through Scripture, tradition, and the gifts of the Spirit. God has given us a great gift for this purpose—the church, the body of Jesus Christ on earth.

THE BODY OF JESUS

God in his compassion touches his people through the very nature of the church. Believers come together, not as a club or business, but as the body of Jesus. They can experience his words, his actions, even his personality in a sense. There are at least five ways the church brings Jesus to the world: as herald of God's Word, as

servant of humankind, as sacrament of God's presence, as supportive community, and as structured institution. God speaks and acts
through all these movements of the body of Jesus.

One of the major threads running throughout Jewish and Christian history is that "God speaks" to his people. In Hebrew Scripture
one discovers that the Lord speaks through creation, the history of
Israel, the leaders of the people, and their writings. But something
always seemed incomplete about these attempts at communication.
The crux of Christian revelation asserts that the Lord went one step
further, speaking through the person of Jesus, God's most powerful
Word: "In times past, God spoke in partial and various ways to our
ancestors through the prophets; in these last days, he spoke to us
through a son, whom he made heir of all things and through whom
he created the universe" (Heb 1:1).

God the Father yearned to speak so strongly that his Word and
love took human form in the person of Jesus Christ, his Son. Therefore, when the church gathers, you should expect to meet, hear, and
touch Jesus Christ.

Our family had a powerful experience of Jesus through my
wife's grandfather. He had a heart attack and was hospitalized for
several weeks at the end of Lent, making those weeks a real time of
sacrifice. Then one day as we were expecting his recovery, he died
of a second heart attack. The day for his funeral fell on Good Friday. The barren church — and the fact that there could be no Mass—
threw us back on our dependence on Jesus and the powerful beauty
and hope in his cross. Her grandfather's death, when seen through
the death of Jesus, spoke very deeply.

HOW DOES THIS LEAD ME TO JESUS?

A good test of what you think God might be saying through
the church is, "How does this lead me to Jesus?" Jesus is the will of
God, so something that leads away from Christ is surely not of God.
"Whoever acknowledges that Jesus is the Son of God, God remains
in him and he in God" (1 Jn 4:15).

Jesus gives you the church in order to draw you into his life.
You are called with Jesus to embody and to speak God's messages
to others within the church. Then a shared life of holiness sends

you outward as a witness to the world.

This mission to speak, act, and be Jesus to the world was not given to a collection of individuals, but rather to the church as the body of Christ after the resurrection and ascension. The Holy Spirit empowers the church to speak Jesus' and the Father's will to the nations, and in doing so, to share the good news of Scripture (see I Cor 12:12-13).

THE CHURCH: HERALD OF GOD'S WORD

Historically speaking, Jesus left behind no writings. Christ rose from the dead in about A.D. 29. He left his followers with the distinct impression that his return and the world's end would happen momentarily. What he did leave behind was his Spirit and the apostles, the church. All that he said was transmitted orally by those disciples to the ancient world. The church spoke and lived Christ to the nations, responding to its mission given by Jesus. Early Christians were Jews.

Then, slowly, early church leaders realized that Jesus was not coming back in their generation. Problems arose in various communities, and the apostles and other leaders needed to interpret Christ's teaching to meet these situations. St. Paul's letters to the Thessalonians (A.D. 51) are considered to be the first writings of the New Testament. St. Mark's Gospel (A.D. 65) is accepted as the first gospel. From A.D. 51 to roughly A.D. 115 the rest of the writings called the New Testament came into being. Each book was a response to communities of believers and their need to apply Christ's teaching to their present situations. They needed help with structures and attitudes.

The point is that Jesus Christ did not leave behind the New Testament, in the strictest sense. He left the church as his spokesperson. The living church then wrote the New Testament. Therefore, the church has the God-given commission to speak for him and to offer interpretation of Scripture. The church would not add anything to the "public revelation" of Jesus Christ contained therein. Rather, the church retains the mission to interpret, clarify, and apply the message of Christian revelation to the current age.

God speaks in, with, and through the church to the world. It is not the only way he speaks, but it is an essential way. The church acts as a system of checks and balances on all the other ways God speaks. With a history and living memory of almost two thousand years, the church has a cultivated gift for helping believers know if a message is in accord with Scripture:

> We allow no authority but the word of God, written or unwritten: and maintain that the control so necessary over the latter exists in... the church, which has been appointed by God to take charge of and keep safe these doctrines committed to her from the beginning, to be taught at all times to all nations. (Cardinal Nicholas Wiseman, d. 1865)[1]

THE CHURCH AS PASTOR AND TEACHER

The church often exercises this gift of speaking God's word through its institutions of leadership, such as the world's bishops assembled in council, the pope as teacher, the bishop of a diocese, a pastor, or pastoral council. The word "institution" comes from Latin words that literally mean "to make something to stand in." These structures are being built through history to help Catholics stand and hear God's voice.

Often, because of its collective wisdom and experience, the hierarchy of the church is the body best prepared to interpret and respond to the messages of God that you receive. You need the church if you hope to hear the voice of God. St. Cyprian (Carthage, 200-258) goes so far as to say, "He cannot have God for his father who has not the church for his mother."[2]

The documents of Vatican II, official papal pronouncements, pastorals from the bishops, and even the directions you receive from your pastor, are some of the ways that God wants to speak. Pope John Paul II's *Christifideles Laici*, for instance, is not just another letter from an old relative. The American Bishops' pastorals on peace and the economy are not just the boardroom musings of a large corporation. A pastor's call to refocus your life from seeking material gain to gaining the kingdom of God is not just another TV sitcom to be turned on or off.

This is why the saints look to the hierarchy for a clear expression of God's will. St. Rose Philippine Duchesne (USA, 1769-1852) brought the Society of the Sacred Heart to the United States in 1818 only at the behest of the bishop in charge of the Missouri mission field. His words to St. Rose and her companions were proven to be prophetic:

> You have come, you say, seeking the Cross. Well, you have taken the right road to find it. A thousand unforeseen difficulties may arise. Your establishment may grow slowly at first. Physical privations may be added, and those more keenly felt, such as lack of spiritual help under particular circumstances. Be ready for all.... One must plow before one raises a crop. You and I shall spend our lives in this thankless task; our successors will reap the harvest in this world—let us be content to reap it in the next.[3]

She went on to work for thirty-four years spreading the good news of Jesus Christ to pioneers and Native Americans.

It is often the pastor or bishop who helps you to see the needs of the whole body, and even of the whole human family. Like St. Rose Philippine Duchesne, you will be challenged to broaden your vision of God's message to the world through ministry. First, you live it out as a brother or sister of Jesus and of others, for all are children of the Father. There is a special bond between believers:

> Let love be sincere; hate what is evil, hold on to what is good; love one another with mutual affection; anticipate one another in showing honor. (Rom 12:9-10)

THE CHURCH AS SERVANT OF HUMANITY: THE MINISTRIES OF PRIEST, PROPHET, AND KING

A number of years ago, our family moved from Massachusetts to Wisconsin. We decided to use a rental truck to pack and move ourselves. We had been part of a small Christian community in our local inner-city parish for eight years. We asked a few of our friends there to help us pack. On moving day over twenty-five people showed up. They brought picnic lunches and refreshments for everyone. They prayed with our family for a safe journey. Our truck was loaded in less than two hours. People from the neighborhood were astonished by this crowd of believers. Some came out onto the sidewalks to watch and stayed to talk about Jesus after we left. When the Christian community really acts like a servant people, the rest of the world is drawn into God's love. In many official ways the church organizes itself to minister Jesus to others through works of mercy, through action for social justice, and through evangelization. In our region, Catholics have helped establish several centers providing food and shelter for the homeless. Our church seeks ways to minister the love of Jesus to AIDS victims, to the handicapped, the elderly, and the homebound. Our diocese fights vigorously in the political and business arenas for adequate, affordable housing.

In their pastoral letters, the American bishops challenge social and economic structures that devalue human life, threaten peace, and deny Christ's preferential option for the poor. Parishes hope to bring others to a living, active faith in Jesus Christ through Catholic schools, religious education programs, adult religious education, retreats, Bible studies, prayer meetings, and healing services:

> When the love of God has taken possession of a soul, it produces an insatiable yearning to work for the beloved—so much so, that no matter how much is done and no matter how much time is spent in his service, it all seems nothing. (St. John Chrysostom, Syria, c. 347-407)[4]

Priest. As you respond to human needs, or rather as Jesus responds through you, you live out the roles of Jesus. First, Christ ministered as priest. He sought to sanctify people and help them enter God's presence. Therefore, you are part of a priestly people. Led and guided by the ordained clergy, you are called to sanctify your family, workplace, your entire secular environment. As Vatican Council II explained so well:

> For their work, prayers, and apostolic endeavors, their ordinary married and family life, their daily labor, their mental and physical relaxation, if carried out in the Spirit—all of these become spiritual sacrifices acceptable to God through Jesus

Christ (cf. 1 Pt 2:5). During the celebration of the Eucharist, these sacrifices are most lovingly offered to the Father along with the Lord's body. Thus as worshipers whose every deed is holy, the lay faithful consecrate the world itself to God.[5]

Prophet. Second, Christ ministered as a prophet. He proclaimed God's message to people, inviting them to accept the love of God the Father and the power of the Holy Spirit to live that love. You are called to proclaim the gospel in word and deed. Pope John Paul II has written,

> You go too. The call is a concern not only of pastors, clergy, and men and women religious. The call is addressed to everyone: Lay people as well are personally called by the Lord, from whom they receive a mission on behalf of the church and the world.[6]

King. Third, Christ ministered as king. He laid down his life to serve those who belonged to him. You can also claim those in need around you through a kingly mission of service. When you aid the poor, the helpless, the sick, and others labeled as useless and unproductive in society, you say yes to Jesus also. You co-create the world with God the Father. As a lay person, it is in the secular realm that you experience your primary call to seek the kingdom of God.

Harold works as a used-car salesman. As a result of a Marriage Encounter weekend, he brings Jesus with him each day to the marketplace. He struggles to tell the truth about each car he is trying to sell. According to him, the profit margin can be inflated by certain practices in buying and selling. He simply refuses to turn back odometers, lie about a car's history, or sell a buyer options and services he or she doesn't need. Harold says, "I don't make as much money as I once did, but I go home each night with a clear conscience, and I sleep peacefully. I have a sense that with each person, I am helping Jesus find the car he needs."

HEARING GOD THROUGH THE CHURCH IN EVERYDAY LIFE

The voice and actions of Jesus come together in his body. How can this affect you in your everyday life and decisions? There are many possibilities. Here are some.

1. Look for the Message of Jesus through Your Daily Life in His Body. St. Bernadette Soubirous (France, 1844-1879) received great graces during the apparitions of the Blessed Virgin Mary at Lourdes, France, during the last century. Her experiences led her to a deeper commitment to Jesus and the church. She entered the Congregation of the Sisters of Charity of Nevers in 1866. She lived the rest of her life humbly accepting whatever happened as from the hand of God and resisted being looked upon as someone extraordinary.

Once when a sister asked her about the apparitions, Bernadette asked what one does with a broom after using it. She explained simply, "You put it behind a door and that is what the Virgin has done with me. While I was useful, she used me, and now she has put me behind the door."[7]

2. Messages from God Will Lead You to Union with the Body of Christ. In June, 1988, suspended Archbishop Marcel Lefebvre ordained bishops for his Traditionalist Catholic movement in direct opposition to canon law. He did this without consent of the pope, and literally drew away from the Roman Catholic church to start his own denomination.

Many people would agree with the former archbishop's concern about abuses in the church. However, Lefebvre's total rejection of Vatican II and the pope's authority cast serious doubt that the inspirations he followed come from God's Spirit. God's true messages bring you into closer union with Christ's body. Further division and fragmentation of the church are not God's will.

By contrast, you see St. Francis of Assisi (Italy, 1181-1226) who faced a church with many more problems than in the present day. Francis and his followers quietly worked and followed God's inspirations. He consulted Rome in founding and revising his rule. His concern for union with the church shaped the Franciscan movement as a long-lasting source of enrichment for the church.

3. Expect God to Speak to You through the Church. God is continuously speaking to you through the teaching authorities and tradition (i.e., councils, creeds, writings of saints, etc.) of the church.

Letters and messages from the pope, your bishop and pastor carry the weight of God's word. They may not be on a par with Scripture, but the Lord wants to speak in his body. Your pastors speak to emphasize or put in "quotation marks" something that God wants you to hear at this time in your life. It is usually a reaffirmation of something you've heard many times before. But now the spotlight is focused upon a particular part of the gospel message. Believers in rich countries today, for example, need to hear God's "preferential option for the poor" emphasized and reemphasized if they hope to live out their Christian responsibilities to the world.

4. Important Messages from God Should Be Submitted to Your Pastor. The apostle St. Paul (d.c. 65) made a point of submitting the major leadings of his life to the church in Jerusalem. (Gal 1:18f; Acts 9:23-31; 15:1-12f). St. Teresa of Avila (Spain, 1499-1569) always brought major moves for expansion of her order to her spiritual director. St. Gemma Galgani (Italy, 1878-1903) even submitted her charism of the stigmata (i.e., visible marks like those suffered by Jesus during his crucifixion) to her spiritual director. Three years before her death, her director told her not to accept this gift any longer. She prayed for the stigmata to cease, and they did.

5. Your Reading of Scripture Should Be Submitted to the Church. One's personal interpretation of Scripture is not to be absolutized. The only way the messages you receive from Scripture can be properly channeled is by seeing if they square with the authoritative teaching of the church. It is also helpful to check the research and views of reputable Scripture scholars. You would do well to read and digest Vatican Council II's *Dogmatic Constitution on Divine Revelation*. A Catholic version of the Bible with good introductions and footnotes is helpful. Also you will want to check your understandings of particular passages with approved Catholic commentaries.

6. Live Your Life in Jesus: Priest, Prophet, and King. Pope John XXIII (Italy, 1881-1963) compared the Christian to a living Bible. You can ask yourself, "What kind of message do others read from my life? Do they see and hear Jesus? How do I participate in the priestly, prophetic, and kingly roles of Jesus?"

Our first apartment on Long Island was a source of scandal and astonishment to people I work with in the church. When the realtor found our apartment she apologized. At the rent we could afford, she could only find us a basement in an integrated area. Catholic friends warned us about the neighborhood.

We were delighted. We felt as if we were returning to a familiar community. For the first ten years of our marriage, we lived in an inner-city neighborhood where there were many different nationalities. We missed our life there, and realized that we were called to live prophetically before the church and the world. God has made us all brothers and sisters in him regardless of language or race. Catholics must "be" God's message to others if we hope to preach that message.

Pope Paul VI seemed to be referring to this kind of cooperation with Jesus in his roles as priest, prophet, and king when he wrote:

> Modern man listens more willingly to witnesses than to teachers, and if he does listen to teachers, it is because they are witnesses.... It is therefore primarily by her conduct and by her life that the Church will evangelize the world.[8]

One of the essential ways God speaks to us is through the church, the body of Christ on earth. Jesus Christ is the message the church speaks to us and through us to the world. As we allow ourselves to be knit together with the other members of his body, we will become heralds of God's Word, servants of humanity, and sacraments of his presence. We need the church to govern, guide, and inspire us as we go forth in ministry to serve in Jesus' name. As Jesus is the total Word of God to the world, we are "little" words of God. We are meant to carry Jesus to our homes, neighborhoods, and workplaces in the concrete actions of everyday life. Then the life and words of Jesus will coincide with ours.

With this chapter we conclude Part Two of this book. We have explored ways that God speaks in daily life, such as wisdom, spiritual identity, circumstances, prophetic inspirations, saints, and the church. All the ways God speaks are important. But what is critical is that we hear the Lord and live according to his spoken love. We believe, as Catholics, that the church is divinely ordained to guide us in hearing and acting on God's word.

FOR REFLECTION, APPLICATION, AND DISCUSSION

Personal Reflection:

1. Recall a time when something said or done by the pope, a bishop, or a pastor really struck you as coming from God. What changes or decisions were you challenged to make in response?

2. How have you experienced Jesus Christ loving you through people in your parish or small Christian support group?

3. Jesus ministers to and through us in the roles of priest, prophet, and king. Which of these roles is closest to your experience of Jesus? Why? Which would be the most natural role for you to participate in as you serve others with him?

Practical Application:

Your experience of the church helps to shape your faith:

1. Recall your favorite parish, and then list three things you liked about it. Spend a few moments thanking God for these specific blessings.

2. Then recall the most difficult parish you have lived in. Simply close your eyes and picture the worst thing that happened. Try to remember the physical surroundings, people, events, and your feelings.

  a. Forgive the people who hurt you from that parish one by one.

  b. Repent of any ways that you acted wrongly or without love. You may even want to bring these matters to the sacrament of reconciliation.

c. To the best of your ability, attempt to repair broken relationships with individual people which resulted from your bad experience. Seek counsel about the most realistic ways to attempt this from a priest confessor or a spiritual director.

You will discover that it is much easier to hear God speak through the church after being reconciled with people there who have in some way hurt you.

For Small Group Sharing or Further Reflection:

1. Describe an important decision you or your family made in the past (i.e., purchased a home, moved to a different area, changed jobs, chose a vacation). How has that decision led you closer to Jesus or away from him?

2. "Let us rejoice and give thanks; We have not only become Christians, but Christ himself.... Stand in awe and rejoice: We have become Christ" (St. Augustine, N. Africa, 354-430).[9] How have you experienced Jesus working through you as you reach out to others?

3. "The church wrote the New Testament." What are your concerns and reactions as you hear this statement?

4. Each neighborhood has a unique character and social makeup. What human needs do you think the church in your particular community is called to respond to?

5. How does God help you experience unity with other Christians in your parish? What can you do in your parish or family when disunity presents itself?

Part Three

Living a Life Open to God's Voice

NINE

Focusing and Centering on Jesus

OUR OLDEST DAUGHTER is an excellent photographer. Over the last several years she has acquired lenses and attachments for her 35mm camera, so that she can take a variety of photos. One of her favorite techniques involves focusing the camera on a single tree or flower, and letting everything else take on a soft blur. Rachel chooses settings and adjustments on the lens to achieve this effect.

Part Three of this book considers the choices that a person makes in order to focus and center his or her life on God. "Focusing and Centering on Jesus" stresses actions that provide a framework for hearing God and living a fuller Christian life. The next chapter, "The Listening Christian," describes attitudes that are pivotal in building a relationship with the Lord.

Mark's professional experience as a cost accountant spills over into other areas of his life. When shopping for groceries, he brings his calculator. He stands at the paper towel rolls, carefully deciding which brand is the best buy of the week. Granted thriftiness is a good trait, but Mark memorizes the price of everything. He complains about the cost of gas and electricity. His favorite question is, "How much is this going to cost me?" Mark doesn't appreciate what he receives in life as much as what he leaves behind. He focuses on the cluttered background instead of the single flower of God's presence.

You may find yourself in a similar situation in your relationship with God. When there is an invitation to live a deeper Christianity, what is your concern? Do you focus on the background and what is to be given up in order to follow the Lord? Or do you focus on Jesus and the joyous new life that he offers when you look to him?

If you wish to hear the Lord's voice, then the first priority in life must be God.

"My eyes are ever toward the LORD,
for he will free my feet from the snare."
(Ps 25:15)

Life itself is redefined. Your thinking must be turned inside out. Only in God comes hope and salvation from sin, death, and Satan.

"With all my heart I seek you;
let me not stray from your commands."
(Ps 119:10)

One passion must consume you—being close to God.

Jesus is a model of this kind of a relationship with the Father. "For just as the Father has life in himself, so also he gave to his Son the possession of life in himself" (Jn 5:26). Jesus and the Father are deeply united. Jesus strives to do what the Father does: "Amen, amen, I say to you, a son cannot do anything on his own, but only what he sees his father doing; for what he does, his son will do also" (Jn 5:19).

As a disciple of Jesus, you are called to live the Father's will in the same way. Your meat and drink, the very air you breathe, should be the Father's will. You are called and empowered by the Holy Spirit to "do everything for the glory of God" (1 Cor 10:31). God created and summoned you for this purpose:

In every good choice, so far as it depends on us, our intention must be simple. I must consider only the end for which I am created, that is, for the praise of God our Lord and for the salvation of my soul. Hence, whatever I choose must help me to this end for which I am created. (St. Ignatius of Loyola, Spain, 1491-1556) [1]

Four concrete means for maintaining a God-centered life are: faithfulness to God's personal word, faithfulness to your vocation, focusing on the needs of the church and the world, and producing the fruits of the Holy Spirit.

FAITHFUL TO GOD'S PERSONAL WORD

One day a group of Franciscan sisters gathered in prayer to ask God's guidance. They expected a prophetic inspiration from the Holy Spirit. The prayer leader began: "Oh Lord God, speak your word to us that we may know and follow your will!" They prayed aloud and sang, then waited in silence for someone to receive a message. Sr. Grace, who was known for her sense of humor, started chuckling. Others glanced in surprise. Then she shared with the rest, "I think God is saying, 'You come to me today seeking my word. That is good. But what did you do with the last word I gave you?'"

God's messages invite a response. Strength is given to take action based on God's word. As you act, a new clarity emerges, purifying your life in a deeper way. Faithfulness itself readies you for new personal messages. All the ways that God speaks are activated by a new vision of the possibilities. Therefore it is valid to ask yourself, "What has God said to me already?"

The Blessed Virgin Mary received God's word at the incarnation of Jesus Christ. Look at her response. She is not just a model of discipleship because she consented to bear Jesus in her womb. The Word incarnate consumed the rest of her life. She was faithful to the message she received. She accompanied Jesus to Cana (Jn 2:1-12) and to the cross (Jn 19:25-27). She even served as midwife for the birth of the Spirit in the church at Pentecost (Acts 1:13-14). Her faithfulness to God's personal word for her whole life serves as an example.

We have been called to God by a particular love that may include personal messages. Shortly after Therese and I married, I sensed the Lord's invitation to enter full-time ministry in the church. I was already serving others as a neighborhood street worker, helping poor families to find adequate food, housing, and health care. All that I learned about attentiveness to human needs became a solid foundation for a career in religious education. One leading built upon another.

My first response to this personal word was to volunteer as director of religious education for St. John's, an inner-city parish. I learned a great deal about adapting programs to address the everyday sufferings and reality of our parishioners. The creativity of the Holy Spirit was my first and primary resource, since we had a budget of under three hundred dollars.

It was sometimes difficult to respond to this new call to ministry. Once I taught a Bible study group for six months with only one participant. But again, faithfulness to the call to teach this one person gave me skills that I still rely on in training hundreds of Catholic Bible study leaders. By God's grace, I am now responsible for a significant part of the religious training and education of thousands of adults—a responsibility which frequently brings me to my knees seeking God's guidance. My own experience convinces me of the importance of faithfulness to God's personal calls.

"Do whatever he tells you," the Blessed Virgin told the waiters at the wedding feast at Cana (Jn 2:5). They poured water into the stone jars, but drew out "good wine" in obedience to Jesus. You are called to take the water of your life and do whatever the Lord tells you. You can't live my call. I can't live yours. But today, you can become more open to God's will for you. Today, you can become the wine of God's word to others.

FAITHFUL TO YOUR VOCATION

A second concrete means toward living a God-centered life is faithfulness to your vocation. Traditionally, the church recognizes three forms of vocation. These are calls to celibate life in priesthood or religious community, to celibate single life in the world, and to married life. Commitment to a state in life is an elusive goal to the world around you. Society may even be hostile to such a commitment. Business and industry often reward only those who put career over family. Sexual chastity is ridiculed as a dinosaur heading for extinction. Our technology threatens the Christian moral values surrounding conception, birth, and child care. In contrast, our Catholic heritage considers faithfulness in a vocation to be a framework for holiness, and the only real context for stable relationships.

Celibate Priesthood or Religious Life. Those who have persevered in religious vocations throughout the changes in the church after Vatican II are often passionate in their sense of God's personal call to serve. One example is Sr. Mary Reparatrice, who works with me as a volunteer administrator for CHARISM, a lay ministry and spirituality institute in the Diocese of Rockville Centre, New York. Sister is in her seventies and has been a member of the Sisters of Mercy longer than I have been alive. After forty years as a teacher and administrator in schools, she began a ministry in the charismatic renewal on Long Island. Her willingness to work in the church and her faithfulness to Jesus are a source of inspiration. When sister finds me discouraged, she offers encouragement. She is a powerhouse of prayer. Sr. Mary leads a large prayer group at Our Lady of Mercy Parish and a diocesan network of over forty intercessory prayer groups. She has boundless hope in the mercy of Jesus, making her a powerful witness to her personal physician, who is Jewish.

When two of his sisters entered religious life, Miguel Augustin Pro Juarey, S.J., (Mexico, 1891-1927) began to seek God's direction for his own vocation. He entered the celibate priesthood as a member of the Society of Jesus. Fr. Pro sought to bring his people to Jesus during the 1920s, a time of religious persecution in Mexico. For two years he secretly ministered God's love and word there, narrowly missing arrest by the police.

Finally, in 1927 Pro was arrested and brought before a firing squad for being a Catholic priest. He forgave the members of the firing squad and knelt to pray. He then stood before his murderers with his arms stretched out like Jesus on the cross. He shouted, "Viva Cristo Rey!" ("Long Live Christ the King")[2] and was executed. His cause for canonization as a saint began in the 1930s. Blessed Miguel Pro illustrates the high call of celibate priesthood which refuses Jesus nothing, not even one's own life.

Living As a Celibate in the World. Living out the call to a celibate lifestyle in order to serve the church and world is a most misunderstood and maligned vocation in our modern era. Can anyone choose the single life for Jesus, without the "pleasures of marriage or the security" of a religious community? Of course, no one of these institutionalized vocations offers perfect bliss. One is not better or less than the other. You should be aware of the incredible challenge that you face in being faithful to Jesus through the celibate life in the world. It is difficult to find a network of supportive relationships like those inherent in religious or married life. You will have to create your own system of relationships for the sake of support and accountability. Yet there are advantages to taking the single life seriously, especially for young adults who are called to prepare for significant careers.

St. Gemma Galgani (Italy, 1878-1903) was seldom in good health. Since her physical strength ruled out the religious vocation of her times, she embraced the single life for God. When her parents died, she took over the care of her brothers and sisters. She constantly reached out to her poorer neighbors, becoming their friend. She refused proposals of marriage so that she could fulfill her call to oneness with God. From her First Communion as a child she recalled, "I realized in that moment how the delights of Heaven are not like those of earth, and I was seized by a desire to make that union with my God everlasting." [3] Though graced with many mystical phenomena—visions, dreams, prophecies, ecstasies, and even the stigmata—St. Gemma lived a normal family life. She served God and others until her death from tuberculosis at age twenty-five.

Before 1971, I thought that people were single only because they couldn't find someone to marry. Madeline taught me otherwise. She lived out a call to teach first grade for thirty years. Her freedom from family commitments left her time for the religious education of children and adults by night. She taught more children, trained teachers, worked on the parish education committee, and took every opportunity to talk to others about God's love and the message of Jesus in everyday situations. She burned for God and God alone. Madeline told me:

> When I decided to remain single for God's sake, I was free for the first time in my life. But what was I free to do? Would I spend my freedom in self-indulgence or in sacrificial concern for others? In response to my baptism in Jesus Christ I have chosen the road of service.

Married Life. The vocation of Christian marriage is a call from God to ministry in the world. How seldom one hears of marriage as such a call. People tend to marry for erotic love, for companionship, for children's sake, and for financial security. All are but a part of the call to Christian marriage. How often do couples marry today for the sake of holiness and service? Each unique marriage is a particular sign of God's love when lived in Jesus Christ.

Christian marriage is a tremendous challenge. Husband and wife can be hard pressed to maintain an exclusive permanent sexual relationship. They must make regular time to nurture their relationship as spouses, lovers, and friends. The weight of work, finances, and child-raising can become burdensome. Little time is left over for individual or family prayer. Spouses must strive to create a network of family and Christian friends who share their religious values and practices, or they will find little support for their vocation.

One striking model of marriage as a vocation surfaces in the Acts of the Apostles and in St. Paul's letters. The home of Aquila and Priscilla served as a beehive of Christian missionary activity. Expelled from Rome for being Jews, Aquila and Priscilla first met St. Paul in Corinth (Acts 18:2-3). They were also tent-makers and shared their home with him. When Paul left Corinth to return to Antioch in Syria, they accompanied him as far as Ephesus (Acts 18:18). Their home became a gathering place for the Ephesian community (1 Cor 16:19), as well as an adult catechetical center. When Apollos, a partly catechized Jewish Christian, arrived in Ephesus from Alexandria, Egypt, Aquila and Priscilla "took him aside and explained to him the way [of God] more accurately" (Acts 18:24-26). When St. Paul wrote about this extraordinary couple, they had returned to the Roman Christian community:

> Greet Prisca [Priscilla] and Aquila, my co-workers in Christ Jesus, who risked their necks for my life, to whom not only I am grateful but also all the churches of the Gentiles; greet also the church at their house. (Rom 16:3-5)

The same call is heard through Vatican Council II. Married couples can embrace their role as the "domestic church," a clear sign of Jesus Christ present in today's confused world:

> Christian spouses have a special sacrament by which they are fortified and receive a kind of consecration in the duties and dignity of their state. By virtue of this sacrament, as spouses fulfill their conjugal and family obligations, they are penetrated

with the Spirit of Christ, who fills their whole lives with faith, hope, and charity.[4]

As Therese and I prepared for marriage twenty-five years ago, we both experienced a call to this vocation. As we have worked and played, made love, raised children, and paid the bills, we have grown in the experience of being "penetrated with the Spirit of Christ." The example of Priscilla and Aquila (as well as other dedicated Christian couples) has led us to give our marriage and family life to full-time lay ministry. This particular call is certainly not God's will for all married couples. Each couple must discern how the Lord calls them to consecrate their love, duties, and vocation to the mission of Jesus in everyday life.

THE NEEDS OF THE CHURCH AND THE WORLD

A third means of living a God-centered life is focusing on the needs of the church and the world. By accepting its role as Christ's body on earth, the church joins in the Lord's mission to the world as priest, prophet, and king. Everyone in the church is called in some way to engage in the works of mercy, social justice, and evangelization within that body of believers.

You may perform works of mercy by collecting food and clothing for the poor and homeless, helping out in a nursing home, soup kitchen, or hospital. Or you may help by donating money to charities like Catholic Relief Services, Bread for the World, or a local food bank. You engage in acts of social justice when you vote for candidates whose platforms are most in line with Christ's teaching and decide to work in campaigns against such evils as abortion, pornography, racism, sexism, age discrimination, exploitation of the poor, and unjust military action. You may work to change legislation which institutionalizes such injustices in society. You evangelize when you live your Catholic faith daily, act with compassion toward all that you meet, and live morally at work and home. Be ready at all times to share your faith in Jesus Christ with those you meet.

Christian life is not a matter of just doing good things, but of doing God-oriented things. There is a call to seek God's will in how you spend yourself. The parable of the talents invites you to consider how you invest your time, treasure, and abilities for the kingdom of God (Mt 25:14-30). You own nothing. All you have and are is given to you by God the Father. Therefore, you are but a broker of your gifts, talents, money, and possessions. Jesus will invite you to look at what you have done with them at the Last Judgment. "Amen, I say to you, whatever you did for one of these least brothers of mine, you did for me" (Mt 25:40).

St. Margaret Clitherow (England, 1553-1586) lived during the reign of Queen Elizabeth I. At that time it was a crime to practice the faith. She became Catholic after her marriage to John Clitherow, a York butcher and meat wholesale dealer. Margaret felt called to meet the needs of suffering Catholics in her country. Though John was a Protestant, he did all he could to protect his wife and their three children from persecution, but Margaret's ministry resulted in several prison terms.

She also knew that her country and her church needed prayer, so she spent almost two hours praying daily before eight in the morning. She fasted four days a week. She met the daily needs of her household and family, but always made time to send food to those in prison. She provided Catholic formation for her children and prayed with them daily. She willingly concealed Catholic priests who were hunted by the government. Her activities finally lead to capital punishment. She was condemned to be crushed to death beneath a giant weighted door on Good Friday, 1586.

St. Margaret's opposition to the unjust laws of her country is quite similar to the work of those who oppose abortion in the United States today. Catholics must actively oppose killing of the unborn. In the considered judgment of many sincere Christians, nonviolent action and even disobedience of certain laws is appropriate and necessary in battling such an evil. Although highly controversial, the "Operation Rescue" movement is a good case in point, where many Catholics risk going to jail by blocking the entrances to abortion clinics in an effort to save unborn babies scheduled to be aborted. Jail terms for these modern Catholic martyrs trying to stop the killing are badges of honor, in my opinion. They honor the memory of saints like Margaret Clitherow, who lived out in everyday life the cost of discipleship to Jesus.

"War hurts flowers and other living things," read the poster on Brian's college dorm wall. That poster and his Catholic Bible caused him unlimited conflict with his family. His father sacrificed a great deal to offer Brian a good Catholic education. As part of a personal conversion during his sophomore year, Brian decided that he could not participate in the military-industrial alliance in the United States, since he views it as unbridled and unjustified militarism.

"Jesus Christ did not call me to build or use guns and bombs," explained Brian, "but to build his kingdom of peace and love." His father, an Air Force major, was deeply hurt. Brian graduated with high honors as a computer programmer. Though many high-tech companies offered him incredible starting salaries, he refused all jobs that were in any way related to the design and construction of weapons of war.

Brian has joined Pax Christi, a Catholic peace organization and sometimes pickets weapons-related businesses. Though his family disagrees with him, they respect his moral courage. Brian takes heart in the American bishops' pastoral, "The Challenge of Peace" (1983), which calls Catholics to work for peace wherever they are.

Patty, a single parent with three children, realizes that she is limited in both time and money as she faces the needs beyond her own family. She chooses one group to send a monthly donation to, the Catholic Medical Missionary Board which supplies medicine for all Catholic missions abroad.

All three people above have taken a responsibility for others in the church and the world. They look outward, doing good for others, not only for themselves. Their attitudes of humble service reflect the attitude of Jesus.

PRODUCING THE FRUIT OF THE HOLY SPIRIT

The fourth way of living a God-centered life is to foster the fruits of the Spirit. Jesus does "only what he sees his Father doing" (Jn 5:19). If you hope to do the Father's will, you must become like Jesus. St. Paul says, "For you have died, and your life is hidden with Christ in God" (Col 3:3). You are called to grow in the personality characteristics of Jesus, known as the fruits of the Holy Spirit (see Gal 5:16-26). The fruits of the Spirit are the results of the power of God's grace at work within you, maturing your personality, and transforming your thoughts, words, and deeds until they are more like those of Jesus. These fruits will not simply fall into your life like overripe apples in an orchard. You are called to participate in their germination and growth by surrendering to the Spirit:

> Put on then, as God's chosen ones, holy and beloved, heartfelt compassion, kindness, humility, gentleness, and patience, bearing with one another and forgiving one another, if one has a grievance against another; as the Lord has forgiven you, so must you also do. And over all these put on love.... (Col 3:12-14)

How can you "put on" or grow the fruits of the Spirit in your life? In his book, *Becoming More Like Jesus: Growth in the Spirit*, Bert Ghezzi describes the following principles that you might employ:

1. Let the Holy Spirit change you so that you might express these fruits to others. Make your life open by total and daily surrender to the transforming power of the Spirit already given you in the sacraments of baptism, confirmation and Eucharist. Decide to do the good and rely on the Lord to give you the strength. Give God permission to do whatever needs to be done to grow the fruits of the Spirit in you—literally to make you a saint.

At age eleven, Maria Teresa Quevedo (Spain, 1930-1950) made a retreat with the other girls attending Our Lady of Mount Carmel Academy in Madrid. She kept a spiritual notebook during this time and made the following resolution: "I have decided to become a saint." [5] From then on she offered little daily sacrifices to the Lord to conform herself to the will of God. She offered up eating a particular food she hated, winning or losing at tennis, accepting headaches and backaches without complaint.

In 1947, Teresa entered the Carmelites of Charity. Before she could even complete her novitiate, she developed meningitis and died. Her cause for canonization has advanced steadily. She was declared Venerable Maria Teresa of Jesus Quevedo in 1971. Her life recalls that of St. Therese of Lisieux (France, 1873-1897) who said:

> This daring ambition of aspiring to great sanctity has never

left me. I don't rely on my own merits, because I haven't any;
I put all my confidence in him who is virtue, who is holiness
itself.[6]

**2. You will come to resemble God as you spend a set time
of personal prayer each day in his presence.** Even five to fifteen
minutes a day is enough to begin the process.

I had the privilege of preparing our son Peter for confirmation
when he was a high school sophomore. As I taught him how to
have a daily prayer life, his rigid and harsh reactions to family members softened considerably. By the end of just a year of daily prayer,
Pete was relating to all of us with much more love and consider-
ation than before.

**3. Turn to God in the midst of trouble and trials, and the
Spirit will transform these problems into spiritual fruits.** God
has a tremendous sense of humor. Suffering is the fertilizer that
causes growth in the fruits of the Spirit.

The first time I asked God to help me grow in the fruit of
patience, I got a big surprise. One impossible person after another
came into my life. As I worked through trying to relate to them
(without committing homicide) I grew in patience with God, myself
and others.

**4. Live your life according to the patterns Jesus Christ has
revealed in Scripture and the church.** For example, Jesus teaches
us to love our enemies.

Once I had a pastor with whom I did not get along too well.
When I prayed about what to do, I sensed that God wanted me to
make him my friend. For the next year I visited him at least once a
month just to spend time together. He died shortly thereafter. The
parish administrator confided to me that I was the only person he
knew of who had been a friend to the pastor during the last year of
his life.

**5. Deliberately imitate those whose lives demonstrate the
fruits of the Spirit.** My wife Therese has taught me a lot about how

to act with compassion toward people who have recently lost a loved one. She believes that greeting them with a hug is entirely appropriate.

I tried this with Lennie, an acquaintance of mine whose only son was killed in a traffic accident last month. Since my hug of sympathy, he has repeatedly reached out to me to become my friend.

6. The moment you realize a temptation to sin, "Just say no!" Refuse to entertain the ideas and feelings connected with the sin. Surrender to the Holy Spirit "prompting you to strike a decisive blow against self-indulgence." [7]

I live in the New York City area where many people's driving habits are pretty treacherous. When drivers on the expressway do something dangerous or just plain stupid, I can easily fall into cursing and condemning them. I am working hard to stop this. Instead I am trying to turn my energy toward intercessory prayer for the driver, asking the Lord's protection and help with the problems which he or she faces.

If you wish to hear the Lord speak, the first prerequisite is to live a God-centered life. Only then will you have a proper focus. Only then will you keep Jesus in sight. Do not allow yourself to be seduced into focusing too much on what you must give up in order to hear God. Focus on Jesus.

Four concrete actions, then, for maintaining a God-centered life are: faithfulness to God's personal word, faithfulness to your vocation, focusing on the needs of the church and the world, and producing the fruit of the Holy Spirit. As you move forward in this way, you will more easily recognize God's voice in everyday life.

FOR REFLECTION, APPLICATION, AND DISCUSSION

Personal Reflection:

1. In your quest to know and obey God's will, do you find yourself focusing on what you might gain or what you might lose? What can you do to focus more clearly on Jesus?

2. God is always speaking. Do you think God could ask you, "What did you do with the last word I gave you?" What one word or sense of direction are you aware of as being unfinished in your life? How should you handle your success or failure in responding to this word?

3. On what two specific needs of the church or the world would you like to focus your efforts? Why are you drawn to each of these needs?

Practical Application:

Living a God-centered life means taking action according to your priorities as a Christian. The following exercises can help you examine and set your Christian priorities:

1. Number your ideal order of priorities from among the following (most important to least important):

___ Family	___ Household	___ Civic (town)
___ World	___ Small support group	___ Personal needs
___ God	___ Church	___Others (be specific)

2. Take an average week from the last month of your life and list the major activities you did under each day.

3. Go back over your average week and estimate the amount of time you spent on each activity. Then make a list of your average week's activities from most time spent to least time spent.

4. Return to your ideal priorities listing. Under each priority, list activities and the amount of time spent. (Example: Personal Needs: sleep [56 hrs], eat [21 hrs], pray [3 hrs], etc.)

5. Make one decision to change an activity based on how your lived priorities (i.e., amount of time spent each week) should match your ideal priorities.

For Small Group Sharing or Further Reflection:

1. What is the quality of your relationship with God the Father? What kind of change or healing would be needed for a richer, deeper relationship with him?

2. What kind of struggles have you gone through in determining your vocation as a celibate priest or religious, a celibate single, or a married person? What helps you to stay faithful?

3. Read the list of the fruits of the Spirit (Gal 5: 16-26). Which two or three have you experienced as the strongest in your life? Which two or three would you like God's help in cultivating? What principle of those listed by Ghezzi for growing in the fruits of the Spirit would help you and why?

4. The church community grows through single, married, and religious vocations. How does your parish benefit from a balance of these Christian lifestyles? What is your response to the shortage of priests and religious in the church at large?

5. "Christian life is not a matter of just doing good things, but of doing God-oriented things!" What is your response to this statement? How is this true in your life?

TEN

The Listening Christian

IT WAS A WARM SUMMER EVENING, just right for a tricycle race at the end of our street. Half a dozen squealing voices sounded through our kitchen window as we ate supper. The baby was still asleep, so we had the leisure to discuss vacation plans with four of our children. As usual, everybody was trying to talk at once. Therese stopped me in mid-sentence as I steered the group to order.

"Was that Katie crying?" she asked.

"How could you possibly hear the baby with all this racket?" I wondered aloud.

She smiled, and replied, "Tim, go stand in the hall and see if Katie is crying."

Off he trudged, returning a few moments later with a whimpering baby in his arms. I was amazed. How could my wife distinguish Katie's voice from all the commotion inside and outside the house?

In the same way that a mother listens for the voice of her baby, God listens for you and knows you. Through the Lord's Spirit you, too, can have the same sensitivity for God's voice. God's voice will become as real as a loved one's call.

The ability to distinguish God's voice amidst the clamor of other influences will become stronger as you grow in your relationship with him. As a mother lives in perpetual availability for her infant, you will become available to God's Spirit. New sensitivity to the Lord will be apparent as you explore wisdom, spiritual identity, prophetic inspiration, the lives of the saints, and the guidance of the church. This sensitivity will yield a new lifestyle marked by docility, patience, flexibility, and detachment. These can become a way of life.

DOCILITY

As a sunflower turns towards the sun, you are invited to respond to the movements of God's Spirit. The willingness to hear and be taught or shaped is called docility. An openness to teaching and correction is important. You may be tempted to say, "Lord, I've had enough. I don't want your word. Don't call me. I'll call you, at my convenience." This is what Scripture likens to deafness, or being like a stubborn mule in God's sight (Ps 32:9).

St. Peter is a model of docility. He is willing to learn, no matter what his own stance or opinion. The Gospels give many examples of Peter's readiness and docility. My favorite episode occurs after he and his companions have been out fishing all night without a catch. Jesus comes along and tells them to go back out. Peter, the professional fisherman, listens to Jesus, the carpenter and preacher, whom he has just met:

> Simon said in reply, "Master, we have worked hard all night and have caught nothing, but at your command I will lower the nets." When they had done this, they caught a great number of fish and their nets were tearing. When Simon Peter saw this, he fell at the knees of Jesus and said, "Depart from me, Lord, for I am a sinful man." (Lk 5:5-6,8)

Peter was able to accept God's word into the depths of his being. This did not always mean that Peter heard correctly. When Jesus tried to explain the nature of his suffering messiahship, Peter balked. Jesus rebuked him sharply. Still Peter was willing to struggle through the process of listening, repenting, then listening again.

Docility is the opposite of a hardening of your spiritual arteries. No matter what your age, no matter how experienced you are in the spiritual life, God can always teach you more. Even if you teach or serve multitudes, you will always be a young disciple of Jesus, the master. He can call out to you with new words at any moment.

I was asked once to give a retreat for a small Christian community. One of the talks was about tithing income in order to support the church in its ministries. This topic had a special message for me, not just my listeners. As I prepared for the retreat, God spoke to me about an inheritance that our family received from my parents' estate. I had been planning to pay off many of our debts and take a vacation. But as I wrote the retreat talks, I realized that God was asking something more.

This leading from God was also evident in an issue of *God's Word Today*, a magazine that I happened to be reading. It was on almsgiving. I then recalled my own parents' generosity. They gave thousands of dollars to Catholic schools, colleges, and orphanages in thanksgiving for a successful milk business. Their example had inspired me to give my own life to full-time ministry. I also remembered a time twenty years before when a woman in our parish tithed an inheritance from her mother and donated it to our struggling family.

This inheritance from my parents was also a gift from God, to be used according to his plans and not just my own. I knew that tithing and almsgiving would play a large role in our use of the money from Mom and Dad. I had a lot more to learn about how to use God's money and goods.

PATIENCE

Most of the time, God doesn't speak quickly or with unquestionable clarity. Understanding God's will usually requires a great deal of Christian patience. An awareness of the Lord's voice comes in stages. It takes time to understand and respond. An individual leading must often wait and mature like a green tomato ripening on the vine.

The technology we live with leads us to expect the opposite. Instant coffee, microwave meals, and vending machines minimize the need to wait. A listening lifestyle challenges you to slow down in much the same way as does "rush hour" traffic, a long line at the supermarket, or the last month of pregnancy. God is not a vending machine, responding to spiritual quarters with immediate results.

It is important to remember, recall, and dwell upon God's leadings and messages. Particular words will unfold and take on layers of meaning in the context of your relationship with Jesus. The Hebrews cherished Yahweh's messages to them in this way. You are invited to dwell on God's word with the same expectant patience and attentiveness:

Take to heart these words which I enjoin on you today. Drill them into your children. Speak of them at home and abroad, whether you are busy or at rest. Bind them at your wrist as a sign and let them be as a pendant on your forehead. Write them on the doorposts of your houses and on your gates. (Dt 6:6-9)

St. Monica (N. Africa, 331-387) lived out a patient kind of faith. Her son, Augustine, abandoned Catholicism and became a Manichean, a member of a pseudo-Christian cult, when he was about seventeen. She spent the next seventeen years yearning for God to act in his life, holding on to leadings and messages about his conversion. Occasionally the Lord would reassure Monica:

A prophetic vision was given Monica.... She seemed to be standing on a wooden beam, while weeping over her son's sinful life, when a celestial being inquired about the cause of her grief. He then told her to dry her eyes, adding, "Your son is with you." Looking toward the spot he indicated, she saw Augustine standing on the beam beside her.[1]

In the early 1970s the Lord seemed to be calling me to full-time ministry in the church. I did not experience clarity about what that meant for me. The only graduate program for ministry of any kind in our area was at Assumption College, Worcester, Massachusetts.

By the time I completed studies for a master's degree in religious education, God had clarified considerably the vision of my life's call. Faculty and advisors had helped me focus my attention on parish spiritual renewal. But after being trained in this way, I still needed a vision of how to proceed. Near graduation day my advisor, Dr. Wayne Rollins, sat me down in his office and asked me what I hoped to be doing in ministry five or ten years later. I described my burning desire to work for parish renewal, as well as the ongoing formation and conversion of adults as disciples of Jesus Christ. Dr. Rollins looked at me and said, "John, I don't think the church will be ready to receive what you have to offer for at least twenty years."

His words had a prophetic tone. My leading would require patience and be tempered by the needs of each parish in which I would work. For the next fifteen years, I was employed as a spiritual counselor, parish director of religious education, evangelist, and adult educator.

With each step the original call was ratified and changed all at the same time. Nine years ago I became the training director of CHARISM. CHARISM is a lay institute of spirituality and ministry under the Diocese of Rockville Centre, New York. It was established by Bishop John R. McCann in 1986 to address the needs and concerns of those seeking to continue their spiritual journeys and further their volunteer and paid ministries in the church and the world. The institute serves over five thousand people a year in regular parish life, as well as in charismatic renewal and other spiritual renewal movements.

Now, almost twenty-five years after Dr. Rollins' prophecy, I am meeting other lay people called to parish counseling ministries, adult catechesis, forming small communities and giving spiritual direction. God is inviting them to patient faithfulness until these needs are recognized by parishes and pastors and used in fruitful ministry.

FLEXIBILITY

Flexibility is an attitude of radical openness to change in response to the Lord's personal messages. At times this means repentance from sin, self-centeredness, or a hardness of heart that blinds you to God's word. At other times it means acting on a leading despite contrary feelings. It can also mean being willing to wait instead of act. If you remain flexible, the desire to please God will temper all else.

When you respond to leadings without flexibility, you may actually rebel against God. You may be tempted to domesticate the Lord's call, tempering what God asks in order to make the invitation more comfortable. In the other extreme, you might become rigid about what you believe God is saying. This can also be a form of rebellion. Abraham thought God wanted him to sacrifice his son Isaac. He proceeded up the hill, but was flexible enough to hear more from the Lord. Your spiritual ancestors, the Hebrews, struggled with flexibility many times. Perhaps it is one reason why they wandered in the desert for forty years.

Though he had a strong attraction to a monastic life of prayer and penance, St. Benedict Joseph Labre (France, 1748-1783) had trouble discerning God's will for his life. His parents thought he was called to the priesthood. He felt drawn to the religious life but tried to remain flexible. Three times he applied to a Trappist community but was turned away. Twice he was rejected by the Carthusians. When later accepted by still another community, he left after six weeks. On a fourth attempt to join the Trappists, he was accepted but had to leave because of poor health. He also suffered from emotional and mental illness. After he recovered, Benedict set out for a monastery in Italy. Somewhere in the Alps God spoke to him:

> He seems to have had an internal illumination which set aside all doubts concerning his vocation. He then understood that it was God's will that he abandon his country, his parents, and the pleasures of the world to lead a penitential life, not in the wilderness or in a cloister, but in the midst of the world— devoutly visiting, as a pilgrim, the famous places of Christian devotion.[2]

His humility, poverty, and union with God gave him the strength to minister to fellow pilgrims, as a kind of street evangelist. Many were brought to conversion and blessed through Benedict. In 1881 Pope Leo XIII canonized Benedict as the "Beggar Saint of Rome."

DETACHMENT

The final characteristic of a listening lifestyle is detachment, sometimes referred to as "holy indifference." This is the willingness to have or not have, to be with others or alone, to cherish or let go, gently living in the presence of God. Work, family life, possessions, needs, feelings, and thoughts are steps in bringing you to God. Even prayer, Scripture, and the disciplines of the spiritual life should be viewed as temporary compared to the union with God that they are meant to foster:

> When the soul frees itself from all things and attains to emptiness and dispossession concerning them... it is impossible that

God fail to do his part by communicating himself.... It is more impossible than it would be for the sun not to shine on clear and uncluttered ground. (St. John of the Cross, Spain, 1541-1591)[3]

Some Christians gain this detachment by seeing life as a journey or pilgrimage into the warmth and security of God's presence. The theme of journey and exodus is important in Scripture. Yahweh leads his people, Israel, out of Egypt and into the promised land. They are purified as they wander from place to place. The writings of St. Luke give a New Testament picture of Christianity as a journey. In Luke's Gospel Jesus ministers first on the outskirts of the nation in Galilee, moving toward the city of Jerusalem and the temple. In the Acts of the Apostles, the church begins in the distant province of Judea and winds up in Rome at the heart of the empire and the known world.

Whether Hebrew or Christian, all believers traveling the road of life are called to be aware of the final destination, which is God. Detachment helps you pay attention to the essentials along the way, with a true appreciation of all things as gifts and expressions of God's love and guidance. Detachment protects you from creating false idols:

In every circumstance and in all things I have learned the secret of being well fed and of going hungry, of living in abundance and of being in need. I have the strength for everything through him who empowers me. (Phil 4:12-13)

Roy and Denise had been married for seven years when they underwent medical tests that confirmed their inability to conceive a child. Therefore, they showered their affection on a family with three small children in their parish faith community. Roy and Denise read them stories, took them to the park, gave them Christmas gifts, and even babysat them several weekends a year. They were the natural ones to be on standby when the fourth child in the family was born. Still, they asked God for children of their own and began to investigate adoption. A two-year wait brought monthly and even daily struggles with detachment. Then baby Christopher came into their life. They were elated.

But Roy and Denise had more love than that to share. They applied to adopt an older child. Instead the agency asked them to consider a brother and sister, seven and four years old. Both had suffered emotional damage and had some learning disabilities. This couple welcomed the children into their family with joy.

KEYS TO DEVELOPING A LISTENING LIFESTYLE

You can take steps to develop a listening heart before God. When God speaks to you, the natural joy in hearing his voice is meant to usher you into self-giving, redemptive suffering, and service in imitation of the master.

1. Embrace a true sense of humility. Humility comes from a Latin word which means dirt. A truly humble person is in touch with his or her dirt. You admit that you are both a child of God, beloved of the Father, as well as a rebellious sinner at times. This honesty about yourself helps you live in a healthy sense of agape love (Greek, self-giving and sacrificial love) toward God, yourself, and others. Avoid false humility that dwells only on your tendency toward sin. Denial of your goodness as a child of God is a denial of Jesus Christ and of salvation.

2. Expect no one else to follow the messages and leadings you receive. If God calls you to share them with others, do not project your response onto them. Even Old Testament prophets could not expect obedience. God warned them to be more like watchmen than rulers (Ez 3:17-21).

3. Judge no one for not following the messages and leadings that the Lord gives you. When Venerable Charles de Foucauld (France/Algeria, 1858-1916) was converted from a riotous life, he received a call to start religious orders:

> The members of these orders would live a life patterned on the life of Jesus of Nazareth. They would go and live among the world's poor, sharing all they had, working each day for a living. They would teach only by the example of living a good Christian life in small groups of three to five.[4]

Charles went to live the life of a hermit in the Algerian desert. After fifteen years among pagans and Moslems in Africa, he had neither converts to Catholicism nor followers for his orders. Yet he remained faithful to his call. In 1916 he was murdered. But since 1933, his gentle love for those so different from himself has inspired the formation of five religious orders and the Focolare Movement in Europe. The fruits came in God's time.

4. Act on messages and leadings after appropriate testing. Chapters eleven, twelve, and thirteen will help you with a process for doing so in important situations. But there are so many little daily leadings that can build up a way of life as you yield to God through them—like greeting a clerk by name, smiling at a neighbor, asking a family member's forgiveness. These do not require discernment, just compassion and genuine concern for others.

5. If others do follow, as you minister in family or church, journey with them as on a pilgrimage. Jesus gives the example of a brother, not a general. Be careful of the images and language you use to share your leadings. This has a tremendous impact. Talk of conquering the world for Jesus can easily lead you into a siege mentality, or threaten others who see themselves as prizes in your conquest. Talk instead about promises you have experienced from the Lord. Have confidence in his personal love for others, while avoiding the use of military language.

6. Look ahead with hope. You must pray, plan, and then act on what you have already heard from God. Live in the present, mindful of God's hand in everyday life. All you can do is offer God the raw material of your particular day, then leave your offering in his hands.

One of the key figures in restoring the Catholic church after the Protestant Reformation was St. Charles Borromeo (Italy, 1538-1584). He served as bishop of Trent and then archbishop of Milan, working to correct widespread abuses among clergy and laity. He experienced bitter opposition. His rights as a bishop were repeatedly challenged. The senate of Milan got so angry that they once barred him from church buildings. A priest wounded him in an assassination attempt. Through all this he had hope for the future:

> He who serves God with a pure heart and, with no thought to any personal and human interest, [and] seeks God's glory alone, must always hope for the successful outcome of his enterprises,

especially when, according to human judgment, there seems to be no hope. For efforts made in service of God are over and above human prudence and depend upon a higher principle.[5]

Attitudes of docility, patience, flexibility, and detachment will sharpen your ability to hear God's voice. Like a mother who recognizes her child's voice even in the midst of noise and confusion, your ears and heart will quicken at the Lord's command.

With this chapter, we conclude Part Three, "Living a Life Open to God's Voice." Now you can begin to consider specific messages and leadings.

FOR REFLECTION, APPLICATION, AND DISCUSSION

Personal Reflection:

1. What two people are you closest to? To which places are you most attached? Name three possessions that you treasure most. How have you given all these to the Lord? How could you grow in detachment?

2. Which scriptural image for a broken relationship with God is most meaningful to you: hardness of heart, wandering sheep, blindness, or being stubborn like a mule? How does this image help you identify your own weakness? How can identifying it help you turn back to the Lord?

3. When shipbuilders look for a sturdy flexible pole to use as a mast, they often select a tall tree alone in a field because it has withstood many storms. How is such a tree like and unlike a Christian?

Practical Application:

Listening to others and to God is an important skill in the spiritual life. "Active" listening involves these operations:

1. Letting go of what you want to say.

2. Understanding the other's outlook and feelings.

3. Repeating what you have heard and the feelings expressed to the other person's satisfaction.

Which of these steps is most difficult for you? Why? Practice active listening for a definite amount of time each week. Try practicing with a partner and ask how you did.

For Small Group Sharing or Further Reflection:

1. Were you more teachable as a child, or are you more teachable as an adult? In what areas of your life are you most willing to learn? What areas are most difficult for you to learn about?

2. What are a few leadings in your life that are presently "sitting on a shelf" in your mind, waiting for another time?

3. "Be willing to be made willing." How does this statement strike you in discussing your own flexibility in responding to God's message?

4. Is following God's will more like traveling on a journey or mapping out a battle plan for you? Why? What do these images say to you?

5. Saints like Charles Borromeo (Italy, 1538-1584) exhort you to seek "God's glory alone" when you try to hear the Lord. Is this an important goal in your life? Describe a situation in which this exhortation would be important.

Part Four

**Responding to What
God Says**

ELEVEN

How Can I Know If It's Really from God?

MILLIONS OF PEOPLE have made pilgrimages to Medjugorje, Bosnia-Herzegovina, since 1981. They are drawn by reported apparitions of the Blessed Virgin Mary to six Croatian youth. Through these young people, many ongoing prophetic messages have been communicated to the world. The Vatican is studying the authenticity of these messages and apparitions, and has neither confirmed nor rejected them.

Between 1981 and 1986 seven young people in Kibeho, Rwanda, Africa, also experienced apparitions and messages they believed to be from the Blessed Virgin. The youths delivered these messages in word, dance, and song to waiting crowds. The bishops of Rwanda have spoken in favor of the experiences, but advised continued study and discernment as to their authenticity.

Other Marian apparitions have since been reported throughout the United States and around the world. The Pittsburgh-based Center for Peace recounts that there are 300-500 active sites where Mary is currently reported to be appearing.

These phenomena have sparked renewal and conversion for many people, based in Marian spirituality. They claim that they are inspired by these apparitions, and some even believe that they are themselves receiving personal messages from God through Mary. They stress the rosary and other devotions. Other Christians are puzzled by the idea of widespread Marian prophecies. "How do I know if these are really from God? Why wouldn't he just speak to us himself?" a friend asks. "Should I be talking to Mary?"

The concern of this chapter is just that. How can you welcome a spiritual message and, at the same time, determine its source and authenticity? This is an important first step as you begin Part Four. Chapter twelve will continue the process by helping you find personal meaning in an authentic message. Then in chapter thirteen, you can examine a process for making decisions based on identifying God's voice through a particular leading.

We will not attempt to affirm or deny any of the Marian apparitions mentioned above. Such an undertaking would be beyond the scope of this chapter. What can be offered is a vision of discernment at the roots of Catholicism. St. Paul's words about prophetic inspiration readily apply. "Do not quench the Spirit. Do not despise prophetic utterances. Test everything; retain what is good. Refrain from every kind of evil" (1 Thes 5:19-22). You are invited to proceed with caution and faith.

Catholic tradition speaks of a gift of discernment given by God for the good of the church. Discernment is a process that focuses the light of faith and love onto a specific spiritual message, state, experience, or action. This charism is concerned with identifying the source of what has been given. It may be exercised by individual laity or clergy, by the hierarchy, or by the entire Christian community. It functions like a Geiger counter, pointing out the presence or absence of God at the heart of spiritual leadings.

Out of 80,000 claims of Marian apparitions reported in the history of the church, only seven have been officially recognized as authentic. When the church's theologians have carefully applied principles of discernment to reported apparitions, they have often discovered an absence of the Spirit speaking in a consistent way. In this chapter, two officially disapproved sets of apparitions in Necedah, Wisconsin, and Bayside, New York, will be contrasted with officially recognized apparitions in Fatima, Portugal, and Lourdes, France.

AN OVERALL UNDERSTANDING OF DISCERNMENT

At the foundation of discernment is common sense. If you want a fresh, authentic orange you must look, squeeze, and even taste one to be absolutely sure. St. Matthew's Gospel exhorts you to use the same principles as you experience spiritual leadings:

Do people pick grapes from thornbushes, or figs from thistles?
Just so, every good tree bears good fruit, and a rotten tree bears
bad fruit. A good tree cannot bear bad fruit.... So by their
fruits you will know them. (Mt 7:16-18, 20)

Good oranges are the result of healthy trees, nutrients in the
soil, proper pollination, and the abundance of water and sunlight. It
is the combination of these gifts and a minimum of bad weather and
disease which yield a ripe, juicy orange.

Something similar is true for spiritual leadings. They are the
result of human nature influenced by the Holy Spirit and are also
affected by evil spirits and original sin. Because you are created by
God and redeemed by Jesus Christ, the Holy Spirit is at work in
you. Even the most evil person in the world is encouraged to do
good. Because of humanity's fall from grace and into original sin,
you have been wounded or warped by a tendency toward sin and
selfishness. Even the holiest person struggles with this inherent
tendency toward evil.

Every spiritual leading is then in some sense affected by the
Holy Spirit, our human spirit, and evil spirits. That is the human
condition. The aim of discernment is to provide the X-ray of a
spiritual leading to determine the strength of each factor. As you
grow in discernment, the goal is to amplify the Spirit's influence,
minimize human interference, and check temptations from Satan.
Discernment leads to deeper surrender to the Spirit and richer, more
nutritious spiritual fruits.

An awareness of the mixed influences behind every spiritual
leading opens you to the gift of humility. "A man is humble when
he stands in the truth with a knowledge and appreciation for himself
as he really is."[1] As you seek the gift of discernment, you will realize the importance of a spiritual director and mature Christian friends.
You need help to know and do God's will. You should walk with a
healthy mistrust of your own judgment, checking with others who
have taken the journey before you. They will help you look at,
squeeze, and taste the spiritual fruits that come from particular
leadings:

My Lord God, I have no idea where I am going. Nor do I

really know myself, and the fact that I think that I am following your will does not mean that I am actually doing so. But I believe that the desire to please you does in fact please you.... I hope that I will never do anything apart from that desire. (Thomas Merton, USA, 1915-1968)[2]

EXAMINE THE FRUITS

In order to discern the authenticity of a particular leading, you must look at its effects on the person who first received the message and others trying to live it out. A leading empowered by the Spirit will produce four signs in these people's lives: God-centeredness, a deeper love for others, living the cross, simplicity of lifestyle.

God-centered. An authentic message will be God-centered. If the focus of the leading is self-centered, then the source is most likely the human spirit or a temptation from Satan. Audrey and Midge first became involved in social justice work during the 1960s. They sensed God's call to work for better housing in a poor inner-city area. Their spiritual directors concurred. At first their love for individual families brought healing. Then they encountered money-hungry landlords and institutionalized racism. Midge and Audrey became enraged and bitter. Less time was spent in prayer, more time in complaining and picketing. Feelings of defeat overpowered them.

Audrey later realized, "The struggle became a personal vendetta. Once I stopped taking time with the Lord, each defeat became 'my' defeat. One day I found myself daydreaming about strangling a certain landlord. I knew I had to get out."

If your focus moves from being God-centered to gift- centered ("my" visions, ministry, charisms), spiritual leadings will also become tainted. Mary Ann Van Hoof claimed she had visions of the Blessed Virgin at Necedah, Wisconsin, beginning in 1949. On August 15, 1950, over 100,000 people flocked to the site referred to as the "Shrine of Our Lady of the Holy Rosary, Mediatrix of Peace." Five years of study and discernment by Bishop John P. Treacy of La Crosse uncovered bad fruits. He issued a prohibition against public and private worship at the site. A reexamination of the case in 1971 by Bishop Frederick W. Freking of La Crosse placed Mrs. Van Hoof and seven leaders of the "Necedah Shrine" under personal interdict, denying them the sacraments (with the possibility of reconciliation) and all services of the church. The following are some of the reasons which were made public:

1. Van Hoof's testimony contained innumerable contradictions and arrogant claims.
2. Her life gave no evidence of the spiritual impact such messages should have had on moral behavior.
3. Van Hoof made venomous and questionable accusations against church and government leaders, antithetical to the spirit of Christianity.
4. She repeatedly circumvented, denied, and disobeyed directives from her lawful bishops.

Van Hoof and her group continued to promote the visions. In 1979 they accepted a schismatic so-called Archbishop Edward M. Stehlik, supposedly of the American National Catholic Church (a sect which broke off from Roman Catholicism).[3] It appears that Van Hoof's spiritual experiences became more important than God's will as expressed through the church and Scripture: "Not everyone who says to me, 'Lord, Lord,' will enter the kingdom of heaven, but only the one who does the will of my Father in heaven" (Mt 7:21).

Apparitions at Fatima, Portugal, in 1917 provide a contrast to those in Necedah. The messages to three children gave warning of dire consequences if the world did not repent and turn to God. The church was urged to intercede for the salvation of the world and consecrate Russia to the Immaculate Heart of Mary. About one hundred thousand people witnessed the sun dance in the sky as a sign from God. A seven-year investigation yielded the following results:[4]

1. There was moral certitude about what had happened.
2. Persons claiming the apparitions were honest, good, psychologically balanced, and respectful of authority.
3. Theological doctrine described was generally free from error.
4. Those responding to the message experienced healthy

religious devotion and spiritual fruits in their lives.[5]

Deeper Love for Others. An authentic message will also draw you into a deeper love for others. Though you need not be perfect, you must be moving toward agape described by St. Paul:

> Love is patient, love is kind. It is not jealous, [love] is not pompous, it is not inflated, it is not rude, it does not seek its own interests, it is not quick-tempered, it does not brood over injury, it does not rejoice over wrongdoing but rejoices with the truth. It bears all things, believes all things, hopes all things, endures all things. Love never fails. (1 Cor 13:4-8)

Aunt Lillie's life radiated agape love. After almost twenty years of a very difficult marriage, her husband left her when she became pregnant. She forgave him and courageously embraced single parenthood when such a state was an unorthodox family embarrassment. She accepted menial work as a housekeeper, caring for other families, houses, rectories, and even a funeral parlor as if they were her own.

At one point she lived with my wife's family, helping out with child care and housework. Her affection and sacrificial love translated into individual outings with her nieces, to buy a special outfit for school or to eat in a restaurant on her day off. After she retired, she moved in with her sister Hattie who was dying of cancer. Aunt Lillie explained, "What else could I do after all the good things God has done for me?"

Living the Cross. The message must bring you more fully into living the cross of Jesus Christ. You are called to make no compromise in your life with sin, the flesh, or Satan. You are called to crucify your pride—to set aside your opinions and even your private revelations if the church discerns them to be out of line. Daily conversion leads to the death of your sinful nature. Mrs. Van Hoof's story above is marked by an absence of living the cross in this way.

A second aspect of living the cross is to be willing to embrace daily suffering. Suffering like that experienced by Aunt Lillie purifies your will. Life may give you a lemon. You have the capacity to accept it as a gift and turn it into lemonade. Lillie's forbearance in a difficult marriage, forgiveness of her husband, and endurance of embarrassment and poverty have transformed her into the image and likeness of Jesus, the suffering-servant Messiah.

Simplicity of Lifestyle. An authentic message or leading should also call you to live the evangelical poverty of Jesus. Through simplicity of life you will realize your dependence on God. Nothing truly belongs to you, except your sin. All else is the Lord's. You are a steward, ready to surrender what you have and to spend it as God directs. Set your heart on God, not on money or possessions.

Such a call is particularly offensive to the typical American lifestyle today. Since the depression and World War II, Americans have been seduced into thinking that they are ordained by God to have not only all they need, but all they may ever desire. While there are reputable Catholic and Protestant television ministries, some popular televangelists seem to live a life based in materialism rather than the gospel poverty of the Lord Jesus Christ. One brand of Christianity justifies this as "prosperity gospel." Some proclaim that those who give money to Jesus will receive a thousandfold back. Some are described as King's kids who travel first class with all the frills.

Now, in a certain sense Christians are King's kids, called to enjoy the goodness and gifts of the Father. But God is speaking *primarily about spiritual prosperity and bounty*, not worldly and material wealth. The promise of a kingdom is true and will be fulfilled, but only fully in heaven, in a much different way than that claimed by some televangelists.

Fr. Ray Bourque, O.M.I., once preached a retreat saying, "No saint has ever lived an elegant lifestyle!" I have wrestled with his statement. It would be so much easier to get caught up into materialism and consumerism than to swim against the cultural tide and choose only the essentials. I've read many saints' lives, searching for just one to prove Fr. Ray was wrong. But even canonized kings and queens offered me no justification. In the midst of their position and wealth, even they sought to live simply, in poverty of spirit and detachment.

In the midst of all the worldliness of a king's court, St. Margaret of Scotland (1045-1093) lived a life of simplicity. Her life was spent in service to the church and in works of charity. She ransomed slaves and gave alms. During Advent and Lent she arose after a few hours' sleep for extra prayer. She took in hundreds of poor, washing and feeding them herself. She committed her personal funds to the support of twenty-four people, as a lifelong service. Bishop Turgot of St. Andrew wrote:

> Not only would she have given the poor all she possessed; but if she could have done so, she would have given away her very self. She was poorer than any of her paupers; for they, even when they had nothing, wished to have something; while all her anxiety was to strip herself of all she had.[6]

One of the greatest obstacles to simplicity is the tendency to define yourself in terms of your actions and experiences. Our Hebrew ancestors in faith struggled with this human predicament. When they left Egypt and slavery, they faced a nomadic existence of desert wandering, always short on food and long on enemies. In the Sinai desert they discovered their attachment to the security of slavery. Later when Moses, Joshua, and Caleb challenged them to cross the Jordan and enter the promised land, they resisted. By then they were attached to desert life, swearing that return to Egypt was better than facing the "veritable giants" (Nm 11:33) who occupied the area. The way to break free of defining yourself by your actions and experiences is to surrender to God's vision of who you are, your spiritual identity (see chapter five). You are an adult child of God, a brother or sister of Jesus. You are unique and gifted because of who you are, not because of what you have or do.

The simple detachment lived by saints contradicts the human tendency to cling. St. Rose Philippine Duchesne (USA, 1769-1852) had the inner freedom to join a different religious order when her first choice failed. Though St. Therese of Lisieux (France, 1873-1897) felt called to be a missionary in the Far East, she was free to concentrate her short life in a cloistered Carmelite house in Europe. St. Frances Xavier Cabrini (USA, 1850-1917) planned to take her sisters to the Far East, but bowed to the pope's request to serve Italian emigrants in the Western hemisphere. She said:

> I will seek to maintain a strict indifference to whatever happy or unhappy events my Beloved may allow to befall me. I will

try to overcome any feelings of disappointment, seeking rather to see, with my spirit, the wise hand of God at work, directing everything that it may turn to my best interests.[7]

UNITY WITH THE CHURCH AND OBEDIENCE TO AUTHORITY

At certain times of the year, if you don't pick up an orange and squeeze it, you will be buying overripe or rotten produce. It is important to look beneath the surface for the attitude of both the person receiving God's message and those trying to live it. What is their attitude toward the church and its authority?

Unity. God is one. The unity of Father, Son, and Spirit is given to the church as a blueprint. You must be living in unity with the church universal (in union with the pope), the local church (in union with the diocesan bishop), and the backyard expression of that local church which is the parish (in union with the pastor).

The mission of the Spirit is to foster that union with the body of Christ. "I am the vine, you are the branches. Whoever remains in me and I in him will bear much fruit, because without me you can do nothing" (Jn 15:5). The meaning is clear. A message or person inspired by the Spirit will promote unity. That which is divisive, causing jealousy, quarreling, and factions is quite suspect.

The Necedah, Wisconsin, apparitions caused serious disunity in a local parish and in the La Crosse diocese. One hundred families were drawn into the sect that formed around Mrs. Van Hoof. By 1979 more than five hundred people had left the church as a result. Even in 1990, some six years after her death, services held at the site of the false apparitions drew hundreds of her followers. The "unity test" did not yield happy results in this case.

Communion with the church is one of the "'Criteria of Ecclesiality' for Lay Groups" described in *The Apostolic Exhortation on the Laity: Christifideles Laici* based on the 1987 World Synod of Bishops. "The communion with pope and bishop must be expressed in loyal readiness to embrace the doctrinal teachings and pastoral initiatives of both pope and bishop."[8]

Obedience. An authentic leading will also promote obedience within the body of Christ. Obedience is not mindless, slave-like or blind adherence to every word the pastor of a church utters. Obedience is an eager process of listening and responding to God's word confirmed through church leaders. Pastors can provide an objective check for believers concerning leadings and messages:

> The trouble with us is we want to serve God in our own way and not in his, and according to our own will and not his.... If we want to become saints according to our own will we will never become saints. In order to really become a saint it is best to do so according to God's will. (St. Francis de Sales, France, 1567-1622)[9]

St. Bernadette Soubirous (France, 1844-1879) received apparitions of the Blessed Virgin Mary at Lourdes in 1858. She lived thereafter in union with and obedient to the church. Mary presented herself to Bernadette as a model of holiness and obedience, the Immaculate Conception. This revelation was seen as "a striking confirmation of the truth of the Immaculate Conception of Mary [occurring] just four years after its definition as a Catholic dogma of faith by Pope Pius IX in 1854." [10] In response to God's speaking to her, Bernadette entered the Sisters of Charity of Nevers in 1866. She lived the rest of her life in obscurity, poverty, humility, obedience, and sacrifice in Jesus Christ. Since then, thousands of people who have visited the shrine at Lourdes have been healed and converted to the Lord.

A contrasting example is the activity surrounding a Mrs. Veronica Lueken of Bayside, New York. She claimed to have experienced visions of St. Teresa of Avila in 1968. By 1970, she believed that the Blessed Virgin was appearing to her regularly. Since then, she has gathered crowds of as many as ten thousand at the site of the Vatican Pavilion in Flushing Meadow Park for further miraculous appearances. According to her, the Virgin desired that a shrine and a basilica be raised on that site and named "Our Lady of the Roses, Mary, Help of Mothers."

A study by the diocese of Brooklyn concluded that the messages contained bad theology, based in a fertile imagination. Mes-

sages which Lueken has received condemned prayer to the Holy
Spirit, misinterpreted the New Testament, and attacked church liturgical practices, like Communion in the hand, as being satanic.
Bishop Francis John Mugavero restated the diocesan position in
1986, asking the group to stop assembling:

> I, the undersigned Bishop of Brooklyn, in my role as the legiti-
> mate shepherd of this particular church, wish to confirm the
> constant position of the diocese of Brooklyn that a thorough
> investigation revealed that the alleged "visions of Bayside" com-
> pletely lacked authenticity... [and are] contributing to the con-
> fusion which is being created in the faith of God's people.[11]

SOUND DOCTRINE AND OPPOSITION TO THE WORLD

To the uninitiated produce buyer, an orange is an orange. To
the gourmet there are differences between navel and valencia oranges. But even the most discriminating shopper must leave all this
knowledge behind and take a bite in order to enjoy his or her choice.
The content of a spiritual message must stand up to the same test. Is
it sound fruit, or rotten and dried-up produce?

Sound Doctrine. The principle of "sound doctrine" has been exercised throughout this book. The content—the insides of messages
received—must be in line with the revelation of Scripture, tradition,
and the teaching office of the church. This test is far more important than miracles or cures in validating a leading. The words of St.
Ignatius of Loyola (Spain, 1491-1556) are apropos in cases regard-
ing the authenticity of private visions and messages:

> To be with the Church of Jesus Christ with but one mind and
> one spirit, we must carry our confidence in her, and our dis-
> trust of ourselves, so far as to pronounce that true which ap-
> pears to us false, if she decides so; for we must believe with-
> out hesitation that the Spirit of our Lord Jesus Christ is the
> spirit of his spouse, and that the God who formerly gave the

decalogue is the same God who now inspires and directs his Church.[12]

In an authentic message, what is revealed by God flows with other doctrine. The Lord cannot contradict himself. An authentic leading somehow makes spiritual sense. This concern for the content of a message brings further clarity when applied to the unhappy situation in Bayside, New York:

> The "messages" and other related propaganda contain statements which, among other things, are contrary to the teaching of the Catholic Church, undermine the legitimate authority of bishops and councils and instill doubts in the minds of the faithful, for example, by claiming that, for years, an "impostor (sic) Pope" governed that Catholic Church in place of Paul VI. [13]

HOW BISHOPS ASSESS APPARITION CLAIMS

In 1978 the Vatican Congregation for the Doctrine of the Faith issued standard guidelines for bishops to use in assessing claims of private revelation. Titled, "Norms of the Sacred Congregation for the Doctrine of the Faith about How to Proceed in Judging Alleged Apparitions and Revelations" (1978), it provides a balanced approach and concrete guidelines:

1) The facts in the case are free of error.
2) The person(s) receiving the messages is (are) psychologically balanced, honest, moral, sincere and respectful of Church authority.
3) Doctrinal errors are not attributed to God, Our Lady or to a saint.
4) Theological and spiritual doctrines presented are free of error.
5) Money-making is not a motive somehow involved in the events.
6) Healthy religious devotions and spiritual fruits result, with no evidence of collective hysteria.

The guidelines are only meant to be used by competent ecclesial authorities (local bishop, regional or national bishops' conferences or the Holy See). The Congregation stresses that the local bishop is the first and main authority in apparition cases. In the most difficult cases, the Congregation becomes involved as well. The Church's final judgment is whether the events are of a supernatural nature or not; there is no mention of Mary in the document.

Opposition to the World. Authentic spiritual messages and the lives of those who receive them will be at odds with the fallen nature and spirit of "the world." Leadings of the Spirit promote peace, reconciliation, chastity, and other fruits of holiness. Faithful disciples of Jesus will live values opposed to the fallen world of rebellion, promiscuity and sexual exploitation, war, power, greed, and self-centeredness. The gospel of Jesus disturbs consciences and is not acceptable to the majority of people.

The test of "opposition to the world" is revealing when applied to the area of television evangelization. Some wealthy, powerful ministries seem to reflect accommodation to worldliness. Other efforts—like diocesan cable stations—generally stand against such a moral quagmire and seek a certain humility even in the midst of fame. They work hand in hand with the National Catholic Conference of Bishops. Authentic efforts to use the power of the media for the sake of the gospel need our financial support.

Catholicism can equip you to discern the source of spiritual leadings. You can look at, squeeze, and taste these messages to search for the voice of the Holy Spirit behind them. Your own common sense will be at the underpinnings of this gift. It is also a gift received by the body of Jesus, enjoyed not so much as a lone individual but in the company of mature Christian friends and a spiritual director.

If leadings, messages, or a person's actions fail any of the tests of discernment, be aware of possible deception and take these leadings with a grain of salt. On the other hand, if a leading meets these tests, there is good reason to respond in the concrete world of everyday life. Quite often leadings will receive a mix of positive and negative test results. Let St. Paul guide you: "Retain what is good. Refrain from every kind of evil" (1 Thes 5:21-22).[14]

FOR REFLECTION, APPLICATION, AND DISCUSSION

Personal Reflection:

1. How well developed is your own ability to discern the spirits behind spiritual messages or leadings?

2. "Every spiritual leading is in some sense affected by the Holy Spirit, the human spirit, and evil spirits." What was your initial reaction to this statement? Why?

3. Who among your past or present spiritual directors or mature Christian friends has been most helpful in teaching you the process of discernment? Why?

Practical Application:

In chapter three, personal reflection question three invited you to write about a situation in your life. After you described what you thought God's will was at the time, you sealed it in an envelope.

Now is the time to reconsider the situation. Without opening the envelope, list any further leadings you have received about the situation since then. Now open the envelope and examine all you have written.

Ask yourself these questions about what you think God is inviting you to do.

1. Will this help me be more God-centered?

2. Will this bring me to a deeper love of others?

3. Does this express openness to the cross of Jesus?

4. Will this reflect simplicity of life?

5. Does the content of the message reflect unity with the church as the body of Christ?

6. Does this reflect a listening obedience?

7. Will this promote freedom from the "fallen spirit of the world"?

For Small Group Sharing or Further Reflection:

1. Signs of a Spirit-empowered life include being God-centered, able to love, open to the cross of Jesus, and growing in simplicity. Which of these is most present in your own life? Which is most difficult for you? Why?

2. Squeezing the fruit or being aware of attitudes behind leadings is important. What temptations do you face in trying to live attitudes based on the gospel? How have your attitudes toward the church helped you achieve obedience and unity?

3. "Sound doctrine" and "opposition to the world" are two discernment tests for the content of a message. Several examples were presented in this chapter. Which story struck you the most? Why?

4. What is the relationship between common sense and spiritual leadings in your own life? How do you use these two elements to verify God's word to you?

5. Discernment is a gift of the Holy Spirit. What gifts have you received from the Spirit? What gifts would you like to experience?

TWELVE

How to Respond to Authentic Messages

MARJORIE READ THE MESSAGES reported to come from the Blessed Virgin at Medjugorje in Bosnia-Herzegovina for years. Though she felt drawn to respond in her daily life to the messages, she could never quite figure out how to apply them. Finally, she decided to go to a spiritual director for help.

Her director invited her to read sections of the universal catechism about Mary's role in the church and the world, as well as about the church's approach to private revelations, such as apparitions. The following paragraphs struck her:

> Throughout the ages, there have been so-called "private" revelations, some of which have been recognized by the authority of the Church. They do not belong, however, to the deposit of faith. It is not their role to improve or complete Christ's definitive Revelation, but to help live more fully by it in a certain period of history. Guided by the magisterium of the Church, the *sensus fidelium* knows how to discern and welcome in these revelations whatever constitutes an authentic call of Christ or his saints to the Church.
>
> Christian faith cannot accept "revelations" that claim to surpass or correct the Revelation of which Christ is the fulfillment, as is the case in certain non-Christian religions and also in certain sects which base themselves on such "revelations." (*Catechism of the Catholic Church*, 67)

She was particularly touched by the thought that it is the role of apparitions and other private revelations "to help [us] live more fully by [Christ's definitive Revelation] in a certain period of history." Marian messages are meant to be like a spotlight that God is shining on a particular part of the message of the gospel or the teaching of the church that we are invited to focus on right now in our spiritual growth. As she discussed this with her spiritual director, she realized that the Medjugorje themes of peace and conversion really bothered her. It was one thing to say that Bosnians and Serbs needed to be reconciled, but quite another to say that Marjorie and her sister-in-law, Kay, needed to patch up their broken relationship of ten years. It was fine to proclaim that the "generic" United States culture must be converted from materialism to Christ, but rather threatening to her to realize that God was calling her to let go of her anger and resentment at feeling cheated by her brothers and sisters in the settlement of their parents' estate.

Marjorie is not alone in clearly understanding God's will and failing to act. Despite your own good intentions, you may find yourself knowing something about God's will for you but failing to carry it out. It is only too easy to stumble into the experience described in the Epistle of St. James:

> For if anyone is a hearer of the word and not a doer, he is like a man who looks at his own face in a mirror. He sees himself, then goes off and promptly forgets what he looked like. But the one who peers into the perfect law of freedom and perseveres, and is not a hearer who forgets but a doer who acts, such a one shall be blessed in what he does. (Jas 1:23-25)

At one time or another, every Christian suffers from this.

Sin. One cause is sin. Satan wants to keep you from living in God's will. If you cooperate with such paralysis and confusion, then you may actually be turning away from God.

Tim and Anne belonged to a small community that was part of RENEW, a parish renewal program which started in the Archdiocese of Newark, New Jersey. When they discussed various possibilities for reaching out to inactive Catholics and the "unchurched," they couldn't agree on a plan. A concern about rejection by their neighbors undermined any attempt to evangelize.

A Fixation on How God Leads or Speaks. Another cause of this inability to act on a clear sense from God is that the spiritual experiences that sometimes accompany certain messages may color them. A focus on ecstatic spiritual experiences like mystical lights, touches, smells, trances, languages, or visions may tempt you to over-emphasize the messages which accompany them. These messages may be from God but do not necessarily warrant a higher priority than messages which come in more natural ways like reading Scripture, studying church documents, or listening to your spiritual director or pastor. It is important to hear God's voice in its fullness. Keep a balance between all the ways the Lord communicates.

Laura frequently received personal direction from God during daily prayer in her basement prayer nook. She particularly sensed God's presence when she burned incense and lit a votive candle before her statue of the Madonna and Child.

Yet one day on her way to work, standing in a crowded elevator, God seemed to be speaking to her about an attitude of resentment toward her husband! Without giving the sense a second thought, Laura dismissed it.

But God pursued her. At daily Mass and in prayer the following day, it became unmistakably clear God had been speaking and wanted her to listen. Never again did Laura assume that God could only speak to her in her prayer nook when she turned to him in daily prayer.

A Sense of Balance. One approach for maintaining a sense of balance about God's word is to focus on the context of messages that are received. If the message is authentic, lining up with the teaching of Scripture, tradition, and the teaching office of the church, there will be several threads running together, weaving in and out. For example, a particular Marian prophecy must be received in relation to Scripture and previous authentic Marian messages like Fatima, Lourdes, and Guadalupe. The Necedah, Bayside, and most other reported contemporary apparitions fall short of this standard. Three important features of these previous authentic appearances serve as a test and support:

1. Mary invites you to be one with God and Jesus.
2. Mary's messages simply reemphasize a part of the gospel

message or church teaching, as the universal catechism notes. 3. Prayer, sacrifice, and reparation for sin are called for.

Even if one particular set of Marian apparitions is declared authentic by the church, a Catholic would not be obliged to believe in them. This is the nature of private revelation. What you hear from God through private revelation provides but one thread in the tapestry of your own spiritual direction.

KEYS TO DISCERNING THE PROPER RESPONSE

Discerning a proper response or series of responses to an authentic spiritual message or teaching is a process of weaving God's word into the concrete reality of your life. In one instance, Jesus uses the image of the sower and the seed to describe this: "But as for the seed that fell on rich soil, they are the ones who, when they have heard the word, embrace it with a generous and good heart, and bear fruit through perseverance" (Lk 8:15).

You can approach a leading as if you were planting a crop. First, you select an authentic spiritual teaching, a seed (like Marjorie's themes of peace and conversion). Second, understand the context, or know what you are planting and where. Third, interpret the meaning. Fourth, consider at least three possible concrete responses. Fifth, evaluate your understanding, interpretation, and responses with mature Christian friends and your spiritual director.

Spiritual leadings seldom fall, fully grown, out of the sky. into your life. Like seeds, particular messages or leadings are dropped into the soil and slowly grow as you live them out. Even at its best, your response to that leading is tentative and reformable. Thomas H. Green, S.J., seems to capture this fragile process:

> God reveals his will to us step by step. He does not give us a total, long-range blueprint of his will for us. Nor does he normally give us infallible advance certainty regarding his will.... The Lord, it seems, wants us to move ahead in faith, to take the next step indicated without seeing clearly where it will ultimately lead us... [There is] the desire to be sure of the landing before I leap, [which] is a quite normal human reaction in the face of risk. Our God, however, does not seem to

want to work this way. He reveals his will step by step and asks us to entrust the future to him.[1]

In order to show you this process of discernment for a particular leading, it may be best to follow one example through my own life. In my experience this process works for both simple leadings and for more important messages from God. However, it is easier to learn with a simple leading.

1. Select What You Think Is an Authentic Leading. In this case I'd like to focus on a spiritual leading toward Marian devotion in my life. Since Vatican Council II in the 1960s, my own personal experience of responding to the Blessed Virgin has flip-flopped a few times. It is a leading which I have responded to at various times of my life and which I have laid aside at others.

I first responded to God with the rosary in grade school. I recall the rosary being prayed over the radio in our home each night around supper time. Our family never prayed it together, however. I would use praying the rosary as a last ditch effort to get what I wanted from God in desperate situations, such as before tests, when term papers came due, when snowstorms were forecast (so school would be canceled), for the recovery of sick relatives, or when nighttime fears struck. The seed of a spiritual leading was present, but it became dormant as I entered my teen years.

2. Understand the Content and Context of the Leading. What does the leading or message seem to be saying in and of itself; what is the content? (This has been considered in chapter eleven.) To whom is it addressed? What is the context? At least three different audiences exist for a particular message. The message may be just for you and your life with the Lord, a personal message. It may be for you and one or more people around you who are joined somehow in the life of God, a relational message. It may be a message for people you serve or minister to, a pastoral message. As a child, the inspiration to pray the rosary was primarily personal.

In my years as a young adult, a different aspect of this leading came to bear. In my junior year of college I made an Antioch Weekend, a retreat developed for young people out of the Cursillo movement. During that weekend, I experienced a deep personal conver-

sion to the person and work of Jesus Christ. I began to help give the
Antioch Weekends. The leader's manual for the retreat suggested
that each team member pray specifically for every single participant. This sounded like a job for the Blessed Virgin and her rosary.
Before each weekend I prayed the rosary daily, offering decades for
team members and individual beads for participants. I was being
led to use the rosary for intercessory prayer. This inspiration was a
pastoral message, since I was praying for those I served and ministered to on these weekends.

When I was twenty-one, I experienced a leading to pray the
rosary from a relational message or leading. I had just broken off a
serious relationship with a young woman. I felt like a failure at
identifying true love. In my pain, I cried out to God for help. One
day I came across a magazine story of a young couple from Ireland.
Each described the search for a Catholic mate. Individually, they
had prayed the rosary for the right person to come into their lives.
After several years of praying this way, they met, fell in love, and
got married. To me, this idea was like a pillar of fire in the darkness.
I immediately began daily prayer with the rosary for God's help.

Among those working on Antioch Weekends was a young
woman engaged to a lay missionary. Her success at evangelizing
other college students, her ability to teach about God, and her prayer
experiences made me jealous. I was dismayed when she and I were
assigned to the same teams several times. After some months, she
broke off her engagement and began dating another member of our
Antioch team. Since we were often working together on retreats,
we began to share what God was doing in our daily lives. I learned
that she, too, was praying the rosary for guidance in choosing a
spouse. What she didn't admit was that in her prayer crusade my
face would often come to mind. Her response at first was to ask the
Lord to get rid of this "distraction." Not too many months later, she
and her "distraction" were married.

3. Interpret the Meaning of the Message or Leading. What does
this mean in the context of other leadings you have received through
wisdom, your spiritual identity, prophetic inspirations, the saints,
and the teaching of the church? Balance leadings with one another.
One leading should not be taken in isolation from the rest of God's

words in your life.

Here I can only admit to an oversight in responding to the inspiration to pray the rosary in my life. After I married, I gave up Marian devotion, seeking Jesus through Scripture instead. I failed to appreciate a new conversion to Christ in the context of what God had already been doing through the Blessed Virgin in my life. It would take a dozen years before I restored a balance with regard to Marian devotion.

In the early 1970s I heard reports of Mary appearing at Garabandal, Portugal. One of the messages, emphasized by Fr. Joseph Pelletier who was a friend and an Assumptionist Marian scholar, was a call to pray each Hail Mary of the rosary slowly and with meaning. Quality of prayer was more important than the number of prayers. Such an inspiration made sense, but didn't call me back to the rosary.

4. Develop Several Possible Responses to the Leading after You Have Interpreted It. I suggest that you try to "brainstorm" three or more legitimate responses to an authentic leading. Why three? In my experience of giving spiritual direction, I've noticed the following principles:

a. Considering only one response can lock you into the "perfect will of God" syndrome.

b. Considering two responses is better, but may paint a picture of God's will as too black and white.

c. Generating three or more responses forces you to think creatively and let go of unproductive emotions. Remember that it is never appropriate to choose a sinful action in the course of discernment. Your goal is a life centered on Jesus. There is an obligation to seek moral clarity so that responses to authentic leadings will truly reflect the Spirit of Jesus at work in your heart.

HOW TO BRAINSTORM POSSIBLE RESPONSES

I have found the following approach helpful in generating concrete responses. First, question the meaning of the leading or message. Then explore resolutions or responses made to similar leadings by believers in Scripture and in the church. The following six questions are helpful in exploring the meaning of a leading for you:

1. What does it say to you or imply about you?
2. What does it say about God (Father, Son, and Spirit)?
3. Is there a command to obey? When? How?
4. Is there a sin revealed for you to confess?
5. What promises can you claim in this leading? What are the conditions?
6. Is there an example you can follow?

Several years ago, I received a letter from a friend who felt drawn to pray the rosary for peace and justice in the world. As he prayed this way, he experienced deepening peace within himself. His sharing tugged at something inside of me. I asked myself the above questions. Question one, "What does it say to you or imply about you?" startled me. He was praying the rosary and discovering deep inner peace from the Lord. I wasn't open to praying the rosary and was in turmoil about finding a new job. At the time, question four, "Is there a sin for you to confess?" showed me that I was prejudiced against the rosary. I thought it was childish or inferior, useful only for intercession. I needed to repent. Question five, "What promises can you claim? What are the conditions?" helped me examine the promise of inner peace from God. If my friend had experienced such peace, maybe I could, too, by praying the rosary. Question six, "Is there an example for you to follow?" reminded me of Fr. Joe's suggestion to pray each prayer very slowly while focusing on Jesus. Then I brainstormed three possible responses:

1. Repent of my prejudice toward the rosary.
2. Pray the rosary slowly each day.
3. Adopt the intention of praying for world peace and justice.

The second phase of exploring responses by others in Scripture and church history was also helpful. This is really an expansion of question six above, but focuses more on your response, rather than the leading itself. Responses made by saints to similar leadings give clues to your own possibilities. Some of the choices that believers have made are:

1. Repent of an attitude or behavior.

2. Forgive yourself or someone else.
3. Work at a particular virtue (Which one? How?).
4. Sacrifice (What? When? How?).
5. Pray more (How? When?).
6. Study more (Scripture, tradition, church teaching).
7. Serve others (Who? When? How?).
8. Wait and expect God to speak more clearly.

The list is not all-inclusive. As you read individual saints' lives, a broader picture will emerge. Some will offer other responses or resolutions for you to imitate. As I applied the above list to my leading about Marian devotion, the following possibilities suggested themselves:

1. Repent of prejudice toward the Blessed Virgin and my own mother, whose name was Mary.
2. Forgive Sr. Mary in grade three for hitting me with her giant rosary beads as she patrolled the aisles.
3. Sacrifice the style of prayer I was using in order to include the rosary. Start in three days.
4. Study about the Blessed Virgin, in order to clear up any misunderstanding. Reread the "Dogmatic Constitution on the Church," sections 52-69, "The Role of the Blessed Virgin Mary, Mother of God, in the Mystery of Christ and the Church." Begin in three days.

TEST YOUR RESPONSES WITH OTHERS

It is important to check out possible responses with others, especially in matters that affect other people. You may want help to see if what you are considering are reasonable responses to such a leading. Would each particular response be helpful to you and others around you? Is it time to act on each response, or are some for the future? With input from my spiritual director, I chose the following actions and wrote them in my journal:

1. Repent of prejudice toward the Blessed Virgin, my mother, and the rosary.
2. Pray the rosary slowly each day, focusing on Jesus, with world peace and justice as my general intention.

3. Study the various church documents on Mary, especially the section on her in Vatican II's "Dogmatic Constitution on the Church."

I reviewed these points periodically over the next few years. My prayer and study have helped me experience two realities described by Vatican II—Mary as the model disciple, and Mary as the mother of believers. I am still growing in my relationship with Mary. As a disciple of Jesus I try to imitate Mary at the wedding feast of Cana, when she instructed the servants, "Do whatever he tells you."

When my mother died a few years ago, I experienced a breakthrough in realizing that Mary was my mother. Praying the rosary has been a special consolation in coping with the loss of my earthly mother.

The purpose of this chapter has been to show you a process for moving from the authentic content of a message to the formation of realistic responses. This process is one way to move towards being a doer of God's word:

> The Holy Spirit writes no more gospels except in our hearts. All we do from moment to moment is live this new gospel of the Holy Spirit. We, if we are holy, are the paper; our suffering and our actions are the ink. The workings of the Holy Spirit are his pen, and with it he writes a living gospel...[to be read on] that last day of glory when it leaves the printing press of this life.[2]

Understand the content and the context of the message in your life and other things God is doing. Is it a personal, relational, or pastoral leading? How should that guide you in responding to it? Generate at least three ways you might respond, evaluating these when necessary. You may want to record these possibilities or treat them as important questions to decide.

In chapter thirteen you will consider the steps involved in moving toward a decision. This process will help you act on God's word, building your life and behavior on rock instead of sand. Jesus encourages you to follow God's voice:

> [You are] like a person building a house, who dug deeply and laid the foundation on rock; when the flood came, the river

burst against the house but could not shake it because it had been well built. But the one who listens and does not act is like a person who built a house on the ground without a foundation. When the river burst against it, it collapsed.... (Lk 6:48-49)

FOR REFLECTION, APPLICATION, AND DISCUSSION

Personal Reflection:

1. At times you know God's will on some level, but fail to carry it out. Two major causes of this are sin and a fixation on "how" God speaks. Which of these two causes have you struggled with in following God? When?

2. Spiritual leadings usually grow slowly, something like seeds. What are two important leadings that developed slowly in your life?

3. (Optional) Return to the personal reflection section of chapter three. There you were invited to examine a specific question or situation. In chapter eleven you were asked to recognize possible leadings with regard to this decision, then check them against the criteria for detecting God's voice. Now choose one of the leadings you think is authentic. Use the steps of this present chapter for developing responses.
   a. Understand the content and context.
   b. Interpret the meaning.
   c. Generate three concrete responses.
   d. Evaluate your understanding and responses with a mature friend or spiritual director.

Practical Application:

One of the ancient Christian tools for developing concrete responses to spiritual leadings and messages is known as a "daily examination of conscience." For the next two weeks, each day as you prepare for bed, take five minutes to do the following.

1. Pray and ask God to enlighten you.
2. Thank God for the whole day, good and bad parts.
3. Review your day. Look at your actions, words, and thoughts, noting where you succeeded or failed in expressing God's love.
4. Thank God for your successes.
5. Repent of your failures and sins. If you note serious sin, resolve to celebrate the Sacrament of Reconciliation as soon as possible.
6. Make specific resolutions to do better in areas where you failed, using a journal as a reminder.

Daily examination of conscience is a powerful spiritual exercise which prepares you to discern the sources of messages and your behavior. God can help you grow in self-understanding and forgiveness.

For Small Group Sharing or Further Reflection:

1. "God reveals his will to us step by step. He does not give us a total, long-range blueprint of his will for us," according to Thomas Green, S.J. How is this statement true or false in your life?

2. How do you feel about your present ability to decide whether a particular leading or message is authentic? Give an example of a situation that prompted these feelings.

3. What kind of spiritual support would you appreciate from friends, a spiritual director, or small group in identifying authentic leadings and messages in your life?

4. Describe an instance when you or someone else tried to respond to a particular spiritual message and something went wrong. What can you learn from this failure?

5. What concrete responses are you presently making to a particular leading received in the past? Would you like to change your response at this point? What have you learned about how you make decisions?

THIRTEEN

Making a Decision in the Lord

MY WIFE AND I HAVE MADE all kinds of minor and crucial decisions in the twenty-five years of our marriage. There was the time we signed a mortgage, committing ourselves to years and thousands of dollars worth of debt. There was the time we decided to take a "second honeymoon," even though Therese was six months pregnant with our fourth child. We have chosen daily family prayer as essential for many years. We have decided on parishes, doctors, friends, books, movies, and Christmas gifts. Some decisions took a long time, others a few moments.

You could probably fill several pages of a notebook with your own list of decisions. It is one of the gifts that you have as a child of God, the ability to make choices. You must move toward what you believe is best. If the Lord has molded your heart and mind, then the process of discernment will be at the heart of your actions. Following God's voice will be essential to you:

> Once the will of God in some matter is known, no matter how hard it may be, it should be undertaken fearlessly and brought to completion regardless of how many or how great be the obstacles encountered. Divine Providence never fails in matters undertaken for his love. (St. Vincent de Paul, France, 1580-1660)[1]

When our family moved from western Wisconsin to Long Island, New York, we had to make some painful decisions about our possessions. In Wisconsin we had a full six-room house with basement and garage. In New York we could only afford a five-room apartment. When you choose God's will as the first priority in your life, it is like moving. Your expectations and plans, large and small, must be reshaped to fit into the Lord's plan. This can be quite threatening. When we left the Midwest, we had to trust God for what could not be taken or owned any longer.

We could not bring our washer and dryer when we moved to New York. The sewer system did not allow such a luxury. Therese was crushed by this aspect of our decision, until she approached it as an invitation to intercede and evangelize in the local laundromat.

The challenge that you face in deciding to follow Jesus is first of all a call to faith. You are invited to believe that God loves you passionately, eternally, and without limit, through all the details of your life. Then every decision is somehow easier and less confusing. You are called to act out a life of constant surrender:

> Fortify me with the grace of your Holy Spirit and give your peace to my soul that I may be free from all needless anxiety, solicitude and worry. Help me to desire always that which is pleasing and acceptable to you so that your will may be my will. (St. Frances Xavier Cabrini, USA, 1850-1917)[2]

The first call you experience is to live a moral life, in line with the gospel of Jesus Christ. You are called to choose the Lord's goodness over sin. The second task involves distinguishing the better "will" of God from among a number of possibilities. You can trust God. The Father has sent Jesus to stand with you; before, during, and after you decide:

> We know that all things work for good for those who love God, who are called according to his purpose.... No, in all these things we conquer overwhelmingly through him who loved us. (Rom 8:28, 37)

A METHOD FOR MAKING DECISIONS

I would like to propose a method for making decisions that has helped me through the last twenty-five years of following the Lord. It is based on *The Spiritual Exercises* of St. Ignatius of Loyola (Spain, 1491-1556). You can remember this method by thinking of four D's: 1) daily relationship, 2) deliberation, 3) decision, and 4) do. There are other approaches. In time, you will develop your own style for decision-making. Hopefully, these four ingredients will be present in some way and might serve as a good starting point for you.

1. Daily Relationship. A daily relationship with Jesus is the foundation of the other three steps for the serious Christian. A personal friendship with the Lord gives you the context for hearing his voice and wanting that voice to shape your actions. Understanding all that is involved in such a friendship has been one of the themes of this book. Now you can review what has been said.

First, you are called to an explicit commitment to Jesus, your Lord and Savior. Second, that commitment can be upheld through daily prayer. Listening and speaking are important in your relationship with God. Jesus wants to hear about the longings of your heart, the joys, pains, successes, and failures. He also invites you to listen to him, to what he shows and teaches you in both direct and indirect ways.

Third, read and pray Scripture for some definite amount of time each day, in order to let your life be shaped by the gospel.

Fourth, consider keeping a spiritual journal. As St. Ignatius suggests, write down what strikes you from Scripture, as well as from events, people, and prophetic inspirations that you may experience.

Fifth, let your relationship with the Lord guide your thinking, feelings, and day-to-day outlook. A good decision is not made on the basis of turmoil or worry. St. Ignatius offers this principle:

> In time of desolation one must never make a change, but stand firm and constant in the resolutions and determination in which one was the day before, or in the time of the preceding consolation.[3]

When Mary was our youngest and had reached the age of four, Therese and I faced the desire to have another child. Both of us were being treated for serious inhalant and food allergies. I was being treated for asthma. We knew there was a 75 percent chance that any one of our children would suffer from the same problems.

Could we knowingly allow this to happen to an unborn child? The agony and barrage of fears were difficult to deal with, especially for Therese. It became very important to bring all this to Jesus in prayer and seek input from other Christians. What we realized as we struggled through this time was that our relationship with the Lord was our primary support. Our confidence in his love would have to be the reason why we would or would not have more children.

Sixth, strive to be honest with yourself and others. You could be deceived. It is important to discuss crucial decisions with others: family, spiritual director, mature Christian friends, even though they may be prone to disagree with you.

Seventh, you need to strive for humility. Be ready for surprises and mistakes as you try to hear the Lord. You may even find that you have given in to sin. Willingness to admit these possibilities will help you repent and grow in your relationship with Jesus. Unless you are open to changing your actions and the reasons behind them, you will have difficulty hearing God. The parable of the two sons underlines the importance of this "metanoia" (Greek: a change of heart):

> "What is your opinion? A man had two sons. He came to the first and said, 'Son, go out and work in the vineyard today.' He said in reply, 'I will not,' but afterwards *he changed his mind and went*. The man came to the other son and gave the same order. He said in reply, 'Yes, sir,' but did not go. Which of the two did his father's will?" They answered, "The first." (Mt 21:28-31, author's italics)

2. Deliberation. The next part of the process is deliberation. It is important to let your relationship with Jesus have an effect on specific choices. Questions arise from many sources. Some come from other people and events, like the father in the parable. Others may arise as you brainstorm responses to a leading. Take the time to think about a decision so that God can speak to you. You may be tempted to take too much or too little time in facing life's questions.

Another thing to avoid is trying to answer too many questions at once. Sometimes one difficult question actually has several questions underneath it that need attention first. At one point we were experiencing a great deal of financial stress due to medical bills. As we asked ourselves how we would pay them, several other questions arose. What kind of a relationship did we have with our allergist? What kind of treatment was most important? Did we need additional part-time work? Should we change doctors?

Decisions and choices usually come in clusters. Look at this example. "Should I join the evangelization committee in St. Matthew's parish next year?" To consider this question it may be important to review previous commitments and decisions. For example, "Should I leave the human services committee or Cub Scouts? Am I spending enough free time with my family? What service are my talents best suited for?" If you experience a cluster of questions, it is helpful to list them. Then consider each one separately.

The next step in deliberation involves seeking a yes or no answer to the most important and specific question that faces you. Don't be afraid to tell someone who has asked you for an answer that you need time to think about your response. It may be helpful to give a specific amount of time by which you will have an answer, so that expectations are clear.

The Ignatian approach suggests writing down the course of

WHAT ABOUT MINOR DECISIONS?

Before going on with the other 3 D's, it is important to distinguish between minor and major decisions. The four D's are best used for major decisions. Minor decisions about what television program to watch, what movie to see, or what gift to buy a friend can be made more easily.

The foundation remains that you are trying to live a daily relationship with Jesus. If something is sinful, it is not an option. There is no need for discernment. If a number of good alternatives are available, which one would you like? Does the alternative fit into your Christian priorities and weekly schedule? If yes, then make your choice and do it.

Suppose you are thinking of going to a movie at your local theater which is rated PG (parental guidance recommended). If there are moral questions to resolve about the movie, you might use the S.T.O.P. approach. S.T.O.P. stands for the following:

1. S.—Seek information and other alternatives. Look up reviews of action that you favor, along with a list of your reasons. To return to the example about joining the evangelization committee, you might write: "I cannot join the group." Sample reasons could be: 1) I'm too busy at work; 2) my family has been complaining about my commitments out of the house; 3) no one ever thanked me for helping with bingo; 4) I don't always agree with the pastor. It is important to write down everything that comes to mind in case there are hidden motives and concerns to bring to the Lord.

When the opportunity arose for me to write this book, I had mixed feelings and unclear motives. It took several weeks to sort out feelings and reasons and then reevaluate my commitments. I brought the proposal to my wife and to my spiritual director. One hidden fear I faced involved dealing with poor spelling and grammar. Could I get help? Therese and I also needed a new agreement about how we would spend time together during the months of writing. Finally, I had to schedule surgery on my right knee to repair two chipped bones. The pain they were causing at that time would have made sitting down to write for long periods impossible.

The deliberation phase is a time to be open and to gather information. After you face your initial response to the question at hand,

---

the movie. What do these suggest about the amount of violence, vulgarity, and nudity contained in it? Look in Catholic newspapers to determine the rating it has received from a moral perspective (if local papers do not carry these, see *Our Sunday Visitor*, 200 Noll Plaza, Huntington, IN 46750).

2. T.—Think about the consequences. Will it brighten or darken your life? Will it weaken your morals? Will it help you to grow toward or away from God?

3. O.—Others' opinions of the movie should be considered and weighed. Did someone whose judgment you trust see the movie? If so, solicit his or her input. Will you offer scandal to family or friends by going?

4. P.—Pray and ask God for clarity about the decision. Take no more than a few moments to an hour in making your decision. Act on your choice and evaluate its effects.

These simple approaches are really only for minor decisions. Don't spend so much time worrying about them that you neglect making crucial and major decisions in your life.

try to let go. Consult those who have a significant stake in the outcome of the decision in a way that welcomes their opinion. How would your spouse or family feel about the change? What do people at work think? You want to ask yourself and others with compassion and respect. The process itself is an opportunity to love. "This is my commandment: love one another as I love you" (Jn 15:12).

To return to the example given, list arguments for joining the evangelization committee: 1) the parish needs you; 2) it will be enjoyable to work for the Lord; 3) you will grow in faith; 4) training is available; 5) you could forgive the pastor for not thanking you and try to work through disagreements. In this particular case, there is input from church documents about the question.

> The presentation of the Gospel message is not an optional contribution for the Church. It is the duty incumbent on her by the command of the Lord Jesus, so that people can believe and be saved.... It merits having the apostle consecrate to it all his time and all his energies, and to sacrifice for it, if necessary, his own life.[4]

When there is input from church teaching, you should take it very seriously, especially in matters of faith or moral behavior. In the example of evangelization, a different outlook on the question is called for. Joining the committee should be compared to ways that you are presently involved in evangelization or other future possibilities. God might use an invitation to join such a committee to challenge you. Do you take evangelization seriously? Is it a part of your Christian life? Why or why not? Would joining such a committee make you a more effective evangelist?

The next step in deliberating involves more writing. Take a clean sheet of paper and write the question you are dealing with across the top, "Should I join the evangelization committee at St. Matthew's?" Then draw a line down the middle, entering pros and cons on either side. Your original motives may still be important to list, plus the other kinds of information you have gathered. Suspend judgment about any one reason until you have recorded them all. You may want to list how this new decision treats Scripture, spiritual identity, prophetic inspiration, your vocation in life, and previous commitments.

Looking at all this may cause anxiety. Be sure and write down feelings also. God wants to touch you and bring you ever more fully into the resurrected life of Jesus. Important questions often call for more time in personal prayer. Deliberation is based in the presence of God. Do what is necessary to dwell in that presence with your needs.

> Free yourself for a little while from your many cares, and take some time to think of God and to rest in him. Enter into your heart and banish everything except your creator and whatever can help you find him. Then having shut the door, say with your whole soul: "Lord, I seek your divine countenance; teach me how to find it again." (St. Augustine N. Africa, 354-430) [5]

3. Decision. In this third phase, the goal is to make a tentative decision, one that you will live with for a few days as a final opportunity for discernment. Evaluate the list of pros and cons. Which are serious considerations? Which are minor concerns? Perhaps you could underline or circle the important ones. For the time being, set aside minor considerations and those that cancel one another out. For example, "not being thanked by the pastor," is taken care of by "forgiving the pastor and bingo committee."

Looking over the list of serious reasons will usually give you a sense of direction. Pros or cons will outweigh each other somehow. Suppose that in going through this process you have had a change of heart. You decide to join the committee. Formalize your decision in some way, perhaps by writing it down or talking it over with your spiritual director or Christian friend. It is a tentative decision. Allow a few days to review the process you have used in case you missed any important reasons to say yes or no. Fast and spend extra time in prayer seeking the Lord. Your decision might still be changed, especially if the person you seek advice from sees a serious issue that you have overlooked.

Prayer should accompany the whole process. But, at this time, it should involve surrender to the Lord. Go before Jesus with your willingness to act. "Lord, here's what I think I should do—join the evangelization committee at St Matthew's for one year beginning this September." Then be still and listen. Record any inspirations or messages. Pay attention to gifts of peace or joy that often accompany a decision made in the Lord. If you experience greater turmoil just contemplating what you have decided, try a second visit to your spiritual adviser. However, don't let this need for peace become the only measure of discernment. It should not be a tactic for procrastinating or escaping difficult decisions. Also keep the tentative decision phase under a week to avoid drawing out the process needlessly.

4. Do. You are ready to act. Make the necessary arrangements to follow through on your plans to join the evangelization committee. Other activities and persons that seek your involvement can easily be refused. Embrace your choice with confidence in the Lord. Pursue it with all your heart, mind, and strength. Treat it as if the Lord had called out to you from a pillar of fire to join that committee. "... Humbly welcome the word that has been planted in you...." (Jas 1:21).

One time I decided to take a job teaching high school religion. There were a lot of good reasons to do it, including the experience in designing new courses. One of the drawbacks was that we would have to live with my wife's parents for two months between jobs. The thought of being in one bedroom with two toddlers for that long was not appealing. What we did not know was that my mother-in-law would only live two more years. Through trusting God, we had the opportunity to enjoy that relationship when we needed it most.

Just ten minutes after Therese and I decided to say yes to the teaching job, I got a phone call. It was a job offer hundreds of miles away in upstate New York. We just smiled and refused it, knowing God had already spoken. All that remained was obedience:

> For by grace you have been saved through faith, and this is not from you; it is the gift of God; it is not from works, so no one may boast. For we are his handiwork, created in Christ Jesus for the good works that God has prepared in advance, that we should live in them. (Eph 2:8-10)

Obstacles may arise to carrying out your decisions. Quite often they are a test of your determination in being faithful to God's will. Teaching high school was very difficult for me, but in the end it proved fruitful. Obstacles can help purify your motives and intentions.

At other times, difficulties show you that it is time to wait before acting. Marsha had decided to quit as head of the women's Bible study. It was best. She would be returning to school, and the group needed a different style of leadership after three years. Her college courses would be starting in a month, but Marsha had not found a replacement. She asked the director of religious education for help and committed herself to an extra two months as leader. It was difficult for her to manage both activities, but it helped the director to get to know people in the group and assess their needs. Members of the group also realized more about what they wanted.

Even the final outcome of your actions must be placed in God's hands. You do not know what will happen. It is God who is in control. Be faithful to your daily relationship with the Lord, deliberating in his presence, deciding by the power of his Spirit, and doing what he tells you. This process can be of value in surrendering new areas of your life to God.[6] Your actions are a very small part of an even larger plan of salvation that will be revealed to the world in the fullness of time.

In Part One of *Following Jesus*, we grew in appreciation of God's voice and word, reaching out in love. Then we explored all the ways the Lord speaks in everyday life in Part Two. There are as many ways as there are people or grains of sand. God's love is without end. Then our attention shifted inward in Part Three in order to paint a portrait of a life open to God's word. Finally, Part Four proposed ways of responding to God's voice and leadings. It may take a month or even a year to become comfortable with all of the tools outlined. The time is not important. What is important is your willingness to live a whole life of apprenticeship as a disciple of Jesus Christ, always ready to listen and respond.

You may want to review the material in this book from time to time. Listening and responding to God is a lifelong process. The important thing is to begin, over and over again if necessary. A desire to glorify Jesus in all your actions can enliven all that you do and give greater depth to your life with each new decision. Start with the basics and draw upon the wisdom and guidance of Scripture, tradition, the church, and the living presence of the Lord's Spirit in all three.

I am still struggling to hear the Lord in different areas of my own life. What courses should be offered as part of CHARISM next year? What does God want me to do about the need for affordable housing for my family? Should Therese and I take a second honeymoon together to celebrate our twenty-fifth anniversary? What should we do to assist Mary with college bills? As we try to come up with a dollar figure, I am torn by conflicting desires. I want to provide her with enough to ease the pressure of loans. I want to foster her financial independence and integrity. And underneath is the question of what it means to parent a young adult. I need God's guidance as I launch my children off into the world.

All of us need God's wisdom and guidance as we struggle to hear God's voice in different areas of our lives. Join with me in making the following prayer for wisdom your own:

Come, Holy Spirit, fill the hearts of your faithful, and enkindle in us the fire of your love. Send forth your Spirit, and we shall be created, And you shall renew the face of the earth.

Let us pray.

O God, who by the light of the Holy Spirit, did instruct the hearts of your faithful, grant that by that same Holy Spirit, we may be truly wise, and ever rejoice in your consolation, through Christ our Lord, Amen.[7]

FOR REFLECTION, APPLICATION, AND DISCUSSION

Personal Reflection:

1. When you face important decisions, are you more likely to spend too much or too little time and thought? Why?

2. Do you ever examine the pros and cons of important decisions? What do you use as criteria in evaluating reasons? How do you try to remain objective when making a decision?

3. How does your ability to trust in God's love affect important decisions in your life? How often do you feel challenged to bring God's will into your choices?

Practical Application:

Use the four D's to answer a question that you face in your life:

1. Consider the situation in the light of a *daily relationship* with Jesus. Clarify the beginning question.

2. *Deliberate*, writing down pros and cons. Include your first reaction, input from others, and leadings from God. Finally, evaluate the reasons, looking for the most important.

3. Make a tentative *decision* for a definite period of time, reviewing it with an adviser if necessary.

4. Make the *decision* final and act on it.

For Small Group Sharing or Further Reflection:

1. Of all the "practical application" sections at the end of chapters, which did you find to be the most difficult? Which was easiest? Why?

2. Why does St. Ignatius of Loyola counsel you not to make important decisions during a time of turmoil, anxiety, or desolation? Does this principle of discernment help you?

3. Have you ever been surprised by the Holy Spirit in trying to make a decision or in the actual results of a decision you have made?

4. God cares as much about the loving spirit behind your decisions as about the decisions themselves. What does this imply about accepting input from family and friends? How can you build relationships while facing important choices together?

5. What is the single most important message or tool you have received from reading *Following Jesus: A Disciple's Guide to Discerning God's Will*?

Resources and Notes

Chapter Notes

ONE
You Can Hear from God Today!

1. Aelred Squire, *Asking the Fathers* (New York: Paulist, and Wilton, CT: Morehouse-Barlow Co., 1973) p. 130.
2. Phil Haslanger, *Stories of Call* (Milwaukee, WI: Hi-time Publication Corp, 1986) pp. 33-34.
3. Susan Muto, *The Journey Homeward* (Denville, NJ: Dimension Books, 1977) p. 64.
4. Pope John Paul II, *Christifideles Laici*, 33 (*Origins*, vol. 18, no. 35, February 9, 1989).
5. Jill Haak Adels, *The Wisdom of the Saints: An Anthology* (New York: Oxford University Press, 1987) p. 58.
6. Adels, p. 60.
7. Adels, p. 67.
8. Material appeared in "The Importance of a 'Study Diet,'" John J. Boucher (Pecos, NM: Dove Publications, 1986) leaflet no. 36.
9. David Fleming, S.J., *The Spiritual Exercises of St Ignatius: A Literal Translation and a Contemporary Reading* (St. Louis MO: Institute of Jesuit Sources, 1978) p. 23.
10. Richard Huelsman, S.J., *Pray* (New York: Paulist, 1976) p. 10
11. *Spiritual Diary: Selected Sayings and Examples of Saints* (Boston, MA: St. Paul Editions, 1962) p. 35.
12. Huelsman, p. 8.
13. Adels, p. 182.

TWO
Why God Wants to Speak to You

1. Anthony de Mello, S.J., *The Heart of the Enlightened* (New York: Doubleday, 1989) p. 151.
2. Daniel L. Schutte, S.J., "You Are Near" (Phoenix, AZ: North American Liturgical Resources, 1971).
3. Solanus Casey, O.F.M., Cap., "Letter to Mildred," *Father*

Solanus Guild Newsletter, vol. 17, no. 3. (Fall/Winter 1987) p. 12.
4. *Apostolicam Actuositatem*, 3, in Walter M. Abbott, S.J., ed., *The Documents of Vatican II* (New York: America Press, 1966) p. 492.
5. *Christifideles Laici*, no. 24.
6. St. Frances de Sales, *Introduction to the Devout Life*, trans. John K. Ryan (Garden City, NY: Image Books, 1972) pp. 215, 218-219.

THREE
What Can Keep You from Hearing God?

1. St. Therese of Lisieux, *The Story of a Soul: The Autobiography of St. Therese of Lisieux*, trans. John Clarke, Institute of Carmelite Studies (Washington, DC: ICS Publications, 1975) p. 259.
2. Donald Bloesch, "Sanctity," *Pastoral Renewal* (July/August, 1984) p. 15.
3. Susan Muto, *Steps Along the Way* (Denville, NJ: Dimension Books, 1975) p. 119.
4. Adels, p. 63.
5. Dinesh D'Souza, "St. Augustine's 'Confessions': Portrait of Redemption," *The Catholic Answer* (November/December 1988) p. 54.
6. William Storey, ed., *Praise Him* (Notre Dame, IN: Ave Maria Press, 1973) p. 25.

FOUR
Think in the Spirit

1. Rev. William A. Anderson, *In His Light* (Dubuque, IA: W. C. Brown, 1979) p. 2.
2. Adels, p. 32.
3. Adels,. p. 13.
4. Mary Reed Newland, *The Saint Book* (New York: Seabury Press and Crossroads, 1979) p. 79.
5. Adels, pp. 172-73.
6. *Gaudium et Spes*, no. 36.
7. Ann Ball, *Modern Saints: Their Lives and Faces*, Vol I (Rock-

ford, IL: TAN Books and Publishing, 1983) p. 285.

8. Adels, p. 155.
9. Jean-Baptiste Chautard, O.C.S.O., *The Soul of the Apostolate*, trans. Thomas Merton (Garden City, NY: Doubleday, 1961) pp. 244-45.
10. Anthony Bloom, "My Monastic Life," *Cistercian Studies*, vol. 8, no. 3 (1973-74).

FIVE
Discover Your Spiritual Identity

1. Fr. Val Gaudet, "A Woman and the Pope," *New Covenant*, vol. 3, no. 3 (October 1973) p. 4.
2. Thomas H. Green, S.J., *Weeds among the Wheat* (Notre Dame, IN: Ave Maria Press, 1984) p. 22.
3. Msgr. Charles Dollen, ed., *The Book of Catholic Wisdom* (Huntington, IN: Our Sunday Visitor, 1986) p. 35.
4. Newland, p. 128.
5. Newland, p. 163
6. Adels, p. 191.
7. Squire, p. 133.
8. *Gaudium et Spes*, no. 36.
9. Greg Gavrilides, "You Aren't What You Feel," *New Covenant*, vol. 8, no. 8 (February 1979) p. 28.
10. Newland, p. 42.
11. Squire, p. 63.
12. 1C, 2E, 3F, 4B, 5A, 6D, 7G.

SIX
Are the Days of Prophecy Gone?

1. *How God Speaks to People Today*, A Nationwide Poll Conducted by The Gallup Organization, Inc.: Princeton, NJ, October 1986.
2. Ball, p. 20.
3. Evelyn Underhill, *Mysticism* (New York: E. P. Dutton & Co., 1961) p. 276.
4. *Catherine of Siena: The Dialogue*, trans. Suzanne Noffke, O.P. (New York: Paulist Press, 1980) pp. 58-59.

SEVEN
Saints: Highway Signs to God's Way

1. Cindy Cavnar, "John Henry Newman: Sermon Selections," *New Covenant*, vol. 10, no. 10 (April 1981) p 14.
2. Tim Slavin, "A Servant of the Cross," *New Covenant*, vol. 14, no. 3 (October 1984) p. 20.
3. Fr. Charles Dollen, *Prayer Book of Saints* (Huntington, IN: Our Sunday Visitor, 1984) p. 144.
4. Ethel Marbach, *Saints of the Harvest* (Cincinnati, OH: St. Anthony Messenger Press, 1981) pp. 14-15.
5. *Lumen Gentium*, no. 50.
6. Adels, p. 43.
7. Boniface Hanley, O.F.M., *Ten Christians* (Notre Dame, IN: Ave Maria Press, 1979) p. 268.
8. Dollen, *The Book of Catholic Wisdom*, p. 122.

EIGHT
Hear God Speak through the Church

1. Dollen, *The Book of Catholic Wisdom*, p. 125.
2. Adels, p. 84.
3. Ball, p. 8.
4. *Spiritual Diary*, p. 227.
5. *Lumen Gentium*, no. 34.
6. *Christifideles Laici*, no. 2.
7. Ball, pp. 71-77.
8. *Evangelii Nuntiandi* (Boston, MA: Daughters of St. Paul, 1975) no. 41.
9. *Christifideles Laici*, no. 17.

NINE
Focusing and Centering on Jesus

1. Green, p. 60.
2. Ball, p. 307.
3. Ball, p. 174.
4. *Gaudium et Spes*, no. 48.
5. Ball, p. 398.

6. Adels, p. 4.
7. Bert Ghezzi, *Becoming More Like Jesus: Growth in the Spirit* (Huntington, IN: Our Sunday Visitor, 1987) p. 148.

TEN
The Listening Christian

1. Joan Carroll Cruz, *Secular Saints* (Rockford, IL: TAN Publishing, 1989) pp. 536-537.
2. Cruz, p. 82.
3. Muto, *The Journey Homeward*, p. 223.
4. Ball, p. 239.
5. *Spiritual Diary*, p. 211.

ELEVEN
How Can I Know If It's Really from God?

1. William Johnston, ed., *The Cloud of Unknowing* (Garden City, NY: Doubleday, 1973) p. 65.
2. Mark Link, S.J., *You* (Niles, IL: Argus Communications, 1976) p. 71.
3. Marlene Malone, "Necedah Revisited: Anatomy of a Phony Apparition," *Fidelity*, February, 1989, vol. 8, no. 3, pp. 8-34.
4. Alan Schreck, *Catholic and Christian* (Ann Arbor, MI: Servant Publications, 1984) pp. 186-187.
5. Robert Faricy, S.J., "The Meaning of Contemporary Apparitions of Our Lady," *SCRC Vision* (April 1989) pp. 8-9.
6. Newland, p. 178.
7. Sergio Lorit, *Frances Cabrini* (New York: New City Press, 1987) p. 181.
8. *Christifidelis Laici*, no. 30.
9. *Spiritual Diary*, p. 91.
10. Alan Shreck, *Basics of the Faith: A Catholic Catechism* (Ann Arbor, MI: Servant Publications, 1987) p. 283.
11. "Declaration Concerning the 'Bayside Movement,'" Diocesan Curia of Brooklyn, New York, Nov. 4, 1986, intro, no. 5.
12. Adels, p. 84.
13. "Declaration Concerning the 'Bayside Movement,'" no. 2.
14. Some of this chapter appeared in "Medjugorje and Marian

Prophecies" (John J. Boucher), *The Love Letter*, vol. 1, no. 3, pp. 8-9.

TWELVE
How to Respond to Authentic Messages

1. Green, p. 96.
2. Jean-Pierre de Caussade, *Abandonment to Divine Providence*, trans. John Beevers (Garden City, NY: Doubleday, 1975) p. 45.

THIRTEEN
Making a Decision in the Lord

1. *Spiritual Diary*, p. 215.
2. Dollen, *The Book of Catholic Wisdom*, pp. 141-142.
3. *The Spiritual Exercises of St. Ignatius* (New York, NY: Catholic Book Publishing Co., 1956) p. 318.
4. *Evangelii Nuntiandi*, no. 5.
5. *Spiritual Diary*, p. 194.
6. Some material from this chapter appeared In "Should I Teach Next Year?" (John J. Boucher) *Religion Teacher's Journal* (April/May 1984) pp. 60-61.
7. Stephen B. Clark, *Finding New Life in the Spirit* (Ann Arbor, MI: Servant Publications, 1982) adaptation of prayer, p. 47.

Related Resources by the Author

An Introduction to the Charismatic Renewal (co-author with Therese Boucher). Servant Publications: Ann Arbor, MI, 1994.

Christian Marriage: Sacrament of Abiding Friendship (co-author with Therese Boucher). Resurrection Press: Mineola, NY, 1995.

Bringing Christ to My Everyday World: Adult Catholic School of Evangelism (author/designer). Audio and video tapes, workbook and leader's guide. CHARISCENTER USA: Locust Grove, VA, 1990, 1991, 1993.

Bringing Prayer Meetings to Life (co-author with Fr. Chris Aridas). Dove Publications: Pecos, NM, 1990.

"Dealing With Common Prayer Problems," leaflet no. 25031-6. Abbey Press Prayer Notes: St. Meinrad, IN, 1993.

Discerning God's Will Day by Day. Audio tapes. CRS of Long Island, Inc.: Hicksville, NY, 1994.

Living Your Christian Priorities. Audio tape. CRS of Long Island, Inc.: Hicksville, NY, 1987.

"Mary's Appearances: Sorting Good Fruit From Bad," *Catholic Update.* St. Anthony Messenger Press: Cincinnati, OH, May, 1994.

New Age Movement: Yes, No, Maybe? Audio tapes. CRS of Long Island, Inc.: Hicksville, NY, 1992.

"Praying the Scriptures Daily," leaflet no. 92. Dove Publications: Pecos, NM, 1981.

Praying the Scriptures Daily: Biblical Spirituality for the 21st Century. Audio tapes. CRS of Long Island, Inc.: Hicksville, NY, 1988.

Prophecy Clinic. Audio tapes. CRS of Long Island, Inc.: Hicksville, NY, 1987.

"Responding to Marian Messages," *Mission Long Island.*

Hicksville, NY, Winter 1994, pp. 4 & 7.
"Should a Catholic Consult a Spiritual Medium?", leaflet no. 47.
Dove Publications: Pecos, NM, 1993.
"Slow Down: God Ahead!", leaflet no. 41, Dove Publications,
Pecos, NM, 1994.
"The Importance of a Study Diet," leaflet no. 36. Dove Publica-
tions: Pecos, NM, 1986.
*You Can Hear From Jesus and Mary: Discernment of Prophecies,
Visions and Voices.* Audio tapes. CRS of Long Island, Inc.:
Hicksville, NY, 1992.

Bibliography

Adels, Jill Haak, *The Wisdom of the Saints: An Anthology.* New
York, NY: Oxford University Press, 1987.
Aridas, Rev. Chris, *Discernment: Seeking God in Every Situa-
tion.* Hauppauge, NY: Living Flame Press, 1981.
Baldwin, Robert, *Conversations with God: A Catholic View of
Prophecy.* Huntington, IN, Our Sunday Visitor, 1988.
Ball, Ann, *Modern Saints: Their Lives and Faces.* Vols. I & II.
Rockford, IL: TAN Books and Publishers, Inc., 1983, 1986.
Catechism of the Catholic Church. Boston, MA: Daughters of St.
Paul, 1994.
Cruz, Joan Carroll, *Secular Saints: 250 Canonized and Beatified
Lay Men, Women and Children.* Rockford, IL: TAN Books and
Publishers, Inc., 1989.
Delaney, John J., *Dictionary of Saints.* Garden City, NY:
Doubleday, 1980.
de Caussade, Jean-Pierre, *Abandonment to Divine Providence,*
trans. John Beevers. Garden City, NY: Doubleday, 1975.
de Sales, St. Francis, *Introduction to the Devout Life*, trans. John
K. Ryan. Garden City, NY: Doubleday, 1972.
Dubay, Thomas, S.M., *Authenticity: A Biblical Theology of
Discernment.* Denville, NJ: Dimension Books, 1977.

Edwards, Tilden, *Spiritual Friend: Reclaiming the Gift of Spiritual Direction.* Mahwah, NJ: Paulist Press, 1980.

English, John, *Choosing Life: Significance of Personal History in Decision Making.* Mahwah, NJ: Paulist Press, 1978.

Fleming, David, S.J., *The Spiritual Exercises of St. Ignatius: A Literal Translation and a Contemporary Reading.* St. Louis, MO: Institute of Jesuit Resources, 1978.

Ghezzi, Bert, *Becoming More like Jesus.* Huntington, IN, Our Sunday Visitor, 1987.

Go and Make Disciples: A National Plan and Strategy for Catholic Evangelization in the United States. Washington, D.C.: United States Catholic Conference, 1993.

Green, Thomas H., *Weeds among the Wheat: Discernment, Where Prayer and Action Meet.* Notre Dame, IN: Ave Maria Press, 1984.

Groeschel, Benedict J., *A Still Small Voice: A Practical Guide on Reported Revelations.* San Francisco, CA: Ignatius Press, 1993.

_____, *Stumbling Blocks or Stepping Stones: Spiritual Answers to Psychological Questions.* Mahwah, NJ: Paulist Press, 1987.

Hakenewerth, Quentin, *Following Your Inner Call.* St. Louis, MO: Marianist Communication Center, 1981.

Hill, Clifford, *Prophecy: Past and Present.* Ann Arbor, MI: Servant Publications, 1989.

Jelly, Fr. Fred, O.P., *Norms for Judging Apparitions and Private Revelations.* Audio tape. Canfield, OH: Alba House, 1994.

La Place, Jean, S.J., *Preparing for Spiritual Direction.* Chicago, IL: Franciscan Herald Press, 1975.

Muto, Susan, *Approaching the Sacred: An Introduction to Spiritual Reading.* Denville, NJ: Dimension Books, 1973.

_____, *Renewed at Each Awakening: The Formative Power of Sacred Words.* Denville, NJ: Dimension Books, 1979.

_____, *Steps along the Way: The Path of Spiritual Reading.* Denville, NJ: Dimension Books, 1975.

_____, *The Journey Homeward.* Denville, NJ: Dimension Books, 1977.

Newland, Mary Reed, *The Saint Book: For Parents, Teachers, Homilists, Story Tellers and Children.* New York, NY: Crossroads-Seabury Press, 1979.

Powell, John, S.J., *Happiness Is an Inside Job.* Niles, IL: Argus Communications, 1989.

Shreck, Alan, *Basics of the Faith: A Catholic Catechism.* Ann Arbor, MI: Servant Publications, 1987.

Spiritual Diary: Selected Sayings and Examples of Saints. Boston, MA: Daughters of St. Paul, 1962.

Stramara, Daniel F., O.S.B., Oliv., *Driven by the Spirit: The Life of St. Frances of Rome with Reflections.* Pecos, NM: Dove Publications, 1992.

van Kaam, Adrian, C.S.Sp., *In Search of Spiritual Identity.* Denville, NJ: Dimension Books, 1975.

Walsh, Vincent M., *A Key to the Charismatic Renewal in the Catholic Church.* Philadelphia, PA: Key of David Publications, 1975.

Yocum, Bruce, *Prophecy: Exercising the Prophetic Gifts of the Spirit in the Church Today.* Ann Arbor, MI: Servant Publications, Revised, 1993.

Zimdars-Swartz, Sandra, *Encountering Mary.* Princeton, NJ: Princeton University Press, 1991.